Reading the Bib

The Pea k's Tail Feathers

Reading the Bible the Celtic Way

The Peacock's Tail Feathers

Kenneth McIntosh

Anamchara Books
Vestal, New York 13850
www.AnamcharaBooks.com

Paperback ISBN: 978-1-62524-495-6
Ebook ISBN: 978-1-62524-457-4

Design and illustrations by Micaela Grace.
Drop cap letters by Valentyn Oleinikov (Dreamstime).
Celtic border by Zfmbek2 (Dreamstime).

CONTENTS

Preface

We must not use the Bible (our ancestors too often did) as a sort of Encyclopedia out of which texts (isolated from their context and read without attention to the whole nature and purport of the books in which they occur) can be taken for use as weapons.

—C. S. Lewis

For my entire adult life, the Bible has been my companion. I have read it on an almost daily basis and its words have influenced me greatly. Now, increasingly I hear people say things like: "The Bible is so awful toward (fill in the blank), so we should be rid of it." Or: "How can you still believe that ancient book when it's used to deny science that could save our world?" I hear this not just from skeptics but also from people in churches. As Lewis feared, the Bible has been weaponized egregiously in our current polarized political climate.

It's hard to see people speak dismissively about something you love. But I must admit, there was a time when I struggled with the same feelings of misgiving toward Scripture. Coming from a background that read the Bible in a hyper-literal manner, Scripture eventually failed to make sense for me. Worse, it seemed to condone some awful behaviors. Reading the Scriptures in the way that I'd been taught, they seemed increasingly less inspired or inspiring.

Thankfully, I didn't stay in this state of disillusionment. Instead, I embarked on a life-changing spiritual journey that was galvanized by my readings from the Christians of the Early Middle Ages, and particularly by the practices of the saints of the British Isles. Insular Christians (the Christians of Celtic lands in the Middle Ages), in connection with their fellow believers in Europe, the Mediterranean, and Northern Africa, developed methods of interpretation that allow the Bible to speak even more powerfully, and more beautifully, to us today.

In the second part of this book, I'll explain these interpretive approaches. First, however, I invite you to journey back in time, witnessing the beginnings of the romance between the Bible and Christians in the British Isles during the Early Middle Ages.

PART 1

The Noblest of Gifts

The Bible in Celtic Lands

One of the noblest gifts of the Holy Spirit
is Holy Scripture,
by which all ignorance is enlightened,
and all worldly sorrow comforted,
by which all spiritual light is kindled.

—Leabhar Brac, *Medieval Irish Manuscript*[1]

ONE

The Gift-Bearers

How the Bible Came to Celtic Lands

Early in the fifth century, Irish slavers kidnapped an adolescent named Maewyn Succat, stealing him from his home in what is modern-day Wales or Scotland. The raiders threw him in the bottom of their hide-covered boat and took him to their land across the Irish Sea. This seemingly minor incident began a series of events that changed world history.

Maewyn had been raised a nominal Christian, but in bondage, his faith increased. Homesick, lonely, he prayed to God more than a hundred times each day. Miraculously, he escaped from Eire (Ireland) and returned to his family and home. More miraculously, he heard God's call to return to Eire, and he obeyed, bringing the story of Christ with him. Most miraculously of all, by the time of his death, Maewyn—now known as Patrick—had persuaded most of the Irish to follow Jesus. He did so simply by walking and talking, treating each person he met with respect.

Patrick left us two written documents: his autobiographical *Confession* and a letter. These are the only existent writings revealing the inner thoughts of a person living in Ireland at that time. Patrick claimed he was poorly educated, but in two short documents he quotes or alludes to Scripture 340 times, citing forty-nine different books of the Bible.[2] It seems Patrick was so immersed in the Bible that its words had fused with his own speech. This meant that as the Irish received Patrick's message they simultaneously received the wording of Scripture.

When Patrick arrived, Ireland was one of the last fully sovereign Celtic regions. Almost a thousand years earlier, cultures with roughly similar linguistic and cultural patterns had conquered most of Europe. The Greeks described these conquerors as *Keltoi*, hence our modern broad designation of "Celts." But at the time of Patrick, there was no sense of "Celtic" identity. Rome had pushed these tribes to the edges of their empire, where they identified themselves by specific tribal or clan affiliations.

Patrick was neither the first Christian to reach Ireland, nor was he the first missionary in Celtic lands. The Britons, under Roman occupation, had received the new faith centuries earlier—hence Patrick was raised Christian. During Patrick's lifetime, the Welsh theologian Pelagius was already famous, both in the British Isles and in Rome.

Patrick was especially important, however, because Saxons advancing across England had brought their beliefs with them, so that much of Britain reverted to older, pre-Christian beliefs. Patrick's influence on Ireland was so thorough that from there the message of faith would rebound throughout the British Isles and then across Europe.

Patrick and his converts saw themselves as part of a universal faith—all of Jesus' followers throughout the world were of "one Savior, one Faith, one baptism" (Ephesians 4:5). They traveled and exchanged manuscripts and correspondences, so that the faith of the British Isles was woven together with that of Continental Europe, the Middle East, and the Mediterranean world.

Yet wherever the new faith engaged with existing cultures, it took on some of the flavor of the local beliefs and customs. Insular churches, far away from the established networks of church control, were even more likely to develop their theology and practices in fresh ways, so Celtic churches developed local and regional variations. For example, many Irish churches affirmed women's equality—despite the fact that there were also Celtic island monasteries that forbade women from even stepping ashore. Some Celtic theologians warned of damnation for anyone outside the church—while others believed all humankind would be saved. For the most part, Christian Celts tended to look at the world from a "both-and" perspective rather than an "either-or" mentality, enabling the coexistence of varying spiritual traditions.

And despite variations in their beliefs and practices, the early Christians in the British Isles did agree on one thing—their great love for Scripture. Celtic Christians of the Early Middle Ages had a deep and reverent respect for the Bible. Patrick declared in his "Letter to the Soldiers," "These are . . . words which never lie: those of God and his Apostles and prophets."[3] The Anglo-Saxon historian Bede, who differed from his Celtic brethren in some significant ways, nonetheless lauded the fact that they "diligently followed whatever pure and devout customs that they learned in the prophets, the Gospels and the writings of the Apostles."[4] According to Celtic scholars Herren and Brown, "British Christianity . . . was governed by a total reliance on the authority of the Scriptures, the corollary of which was a marked distrust of any theology that was not Scripture based."[5]

A legendary incident in the life of a later, sixth-century Celtic saint, Columba, attests to the Celts' intense passion for Scripture (although the story is not flattering of the saint). Columba coveted a copy of the Psalms belonging to a neighboring monastery, but the owners would not let him remove the special book from their library. He therefore set about stealthily copying the text. When his covert scribal work was discovered, Columba insisted that he be allowed to keep his copy of the book. When this claim was denied, the holy man resorted to warlike behavior that has been sadly endemic to Celts throughout history. He rallied his O'Neil clansmen to take up arms against the offending monastery, and when the dust settled, the blood of a thousand Irishmen stained sanctified ground. As a punishment, the synod of Ireland banished Columba from his beloved native land—a judgment that led him to evangelize the Picts (in modern-day Scotland). This tale, though tragic, illustrates the value that Columba and his contemporaries placed on the Bible.[6]

Focusing on Celtic—or Insular—Christianity can be both inspiring and intriguing to us today. There's a certain magic and allure to the word *Celtic*. However, while modern writers often speak of "Celtic Christianity" as distinct from the faith of Christians in other nations at that time, that perspective is more than a little erroneous. The saints of the British Isles had far more in common with their fellow believers around the world than they held distinctions from them.

Notes

1. Martin McNamara, "Love for and Study of the Bible, God's Word, in Early Irish Tradition," in Salvador Ryan and Brendan Leahy, *Treasures of Irish Christianity: Volume II: A People of the Word* (Dublin: Veritas, 2013), 57.

2. Leslie Hardinge, *The Celtic Church in Britain* (New York: Teach Services, 2005), 29.

3. *Patrick's Letter to the Soldiers*, quoted by Oliver Davies in *Celtic Spirituality* (New York: Paulist Press, 1999), 88–89.

4. Bede, quoted by Leslie Hardinge in *The Celtic Church in Britain*, 30.

5. Michael W. Herren and Shirley Ann Brown, *Christ in Celtic Christianity: Britain and Ireland from the Fifth to the Tenth Century* (Woodbridge, Suffolk, UK: Boydell Press, 2012), 106.

6. Joseph Falaky Nagy, *Conversing with Angels and Ancients: Literary Myths of Medieval Ireland* (Ithaca, NY: Cornell University Press, 1997), 147.

TWO

The Gift Received

The Bible in the Early Middle Ages

When we hear the word "Bible," a picture pops up in our minds. We think of one volume, likely bound in leather, containing either sixty-six books (if we're Protestant) or seventy-three (if we're Catholic), written in the language we speak. When we imagine Patrick bringing the Bible to the Pagan Irish, we might envision him carrying a Bible like that. In some ways this would be accurate, but in other respects widely off the mark.

The Physical Book

Judging the Good Book by its cover, early-medieval Bibles would resemble those of today. By the year 200, Christians had begun circulating their scriptures in *codex* form. A codex contains flat pages, sewn together at the spine and encased in front and back covers—in short, the format of a modern printed book. Why did early Christians write their Bible text in codex style, rather than the format of scrolls, used for a millennium previously? Perhaps it was easier for a persecuted faith to guard its message in more compact form, or maybe bound books were more useful to carry when spreading the message of Christ. No one is certain, but by the fourth century, modern-shaped Bibles were common.

The new format also brought a change in materials. The word "bible" comes from *Byblos*, the Phoenician port that exported papyrus to the Greek world. Papyrus was a thin paper made from crushed river reeds pasted together, and early Jewish and Christian sacred texts were often copied onto this material. By Patrick's time, however, vellum—made from carefully scraped calves' hides—was used for pages.

The Canon

At the time of Ireland's conversion, Christians had only recently agreed upon the list of books that constitutes the Bible. This set of biblical texts is known as the *canon*, from the Greek word for "rule" or "measuring stick." For three hundred years after the lifetime of Christ, the Jesus movement debated which books should be regarded as God-inspired scriptures. Some books, such as the four Gospels found in Bibles today, were uncontested. The letters of Paul were also quickly agreed upon. Some early Christians wished to also include in the canon additional books, such as *The Shepherd of Hermas* and the *Epistle of Barnabas.*

Late in the fourth century, a church council and an Egyptian bishop resolved debates over the canon. In 363, the council of Laodicea (in modern-day Turkey) declared that the New Testament consists of twenty-six inspired books, which are still included in today's Bible. The Book of Revelation was excluded, since most Eastern Christians rejected it. However, Bishop Athanasius of Alexandria, Egypt, who held authority over the Eastern churches, added the Book of Revelation in 367.

The Council of Laodicea also decreed the extent of the Old Testament canon, which was the same as the forty-six books found in Catholic Bibles today. This list includes what Protestants refer to as the "Old Testament Apocrypha," books that were later rejected by the sixteenth-century Protestant Reformation.

Celtic monasteries also copied sacred books that were *not* included in either the Old or New Testament canon. The Council of Laodicea had prohibited some of these books, while others were used as devotional reading in Eastern and Western churches. Nowadays they are referred to simply as "Apocrypha" (because of the similar wording, Protestants sometimes confuse these with the books that are included in the Old Testament of the Catholic Bible). Irish scholars translated these books, originally written in Greek, Georgian, Syrian, Ethiopic, and Armenian languages, into their own language.[1]

If you asked Patrick, "What are the authorized and inspired books of Sacred Scripture?" he would likely have listed the same seventy-three books found in Catholic Bibles today. However, it is unlikely that he possessed all of those texts in one bound volume, since early complete Bibles were rare, costly, and so bulky that they were difficult to transport. More common copies of the Bible would contain the four Gospels, and less often the entire New Testament. Monks used the Psalms for daily prayers, so Psalters were also common as bound collections. Other books of the Old Testament would likely have been contained in separate volumes.

Patrick's Bible would have been written in Latin, as were most Bibles in the Celtic lands during the Middle Ages. At the same time that Patrick preached in Ireland, a scholar named Jerome spent decades living in Bethlehem, adjacent to the alleged birthplace of Jesus, translating the Bible from the original Hebrew and Greek into Latin. Paula and Eustochium, two women proficient in Hebrew, assisted him. The Latin Bible that Jerome produced—called the Vulgate ("Common Version")—was the most-used translation in the history of the Christian faith, the standard text for over a thousand years. Jerome's translation reached the British Isles by the mid-fifth century.

There were other Latin translations, now referred to as "Old Latin" Bibles, before Jerome's version. Numerous scholars had made these, and they varied greatly in quality and translation choices. The majority of Bibles in Ireland

and Britain were of this Old Latin variety up until the ninth century; therefore, the Celts read their Scriptures in a considerable variety of translations. The Book of Kells, copied around 800, is a mix of Vulgate and Old Latin translations.

Note

1. Salvador Ryan and Brendan Leahy, *Treasures of Irish Christianity, Volume II: A People of the Word* (Dublin: Veritas, 2013), 61.

THREE

The Gift Returned

Celtic Versions of the Bible

Before Patrick, only the Irish intelligentsia (the druids) possessed written language. This was in the form of Ogham lettering, straight lines carved on stone or wood, used for charms or memorials. The vast body of Irish artistic expression existed in oral form.

As soon as Patrick and other Christians introduced the Latin alphabet and the technology of writing with ink on vellum, Hibernian talents leapt onto the possibilities of these new forms. Celtic cultures had long been intoxicated with words; for them, language was a form of magic—the most potent form.

The most esteemed members of Celtic society were bards. Amergin, the hero who wed the Goddess Eiré and took possession of Ireland from the fairy people, was a bard; and so, according to their mythology, the Irish race was founded upon the arts of word-making. Now, with the intermingling of European and Irish cultures, the Celtic love of language-play could translate from oral to physical form. The Celts saw the pages of parchment as naked canvas, pleading for the artist's brush, so they took the curling, flexible shapes of Latin letters and twisted and twirled them across vellum. Insular calligraphers were so enamored of the shapes of letters that they sometimes also used non-Latin letters in Latin texts if the foreign letters offered more visual opportunity.

For a millennium before Christianity, the great stories of their gods, demi-gods, and heroes had given identity to the Irish clans; now the Irish had a new set of stories, with exotic lands, mighty champions, and the superlative tales of the God-man. People intoxicated with music also had a hundred-and-fifty poems (the Book of Psalms), ready to set to music and sing for the King of Mysteries. Such marvelous words called forth the beauty of visual art to match their wonders; now, the spirals and knotwork and splendid forms previously utilized for carved stones, cauldrons, shields, and jewelry were woven into the playful spell of words on paper. "Looking at all the various forms," wrote art historian and ancient manuscript expert Benjamin Tilgham, "one gets the impression that Insular calligraphers were consciously playing with the fact that a letter can be twisted and abstracted into a seemingly infinite variety of forms and yet still ultimately serve to represent the same vocal sound."[1]

The innovative genius of the Irish also produced a very practical breakthrough in the art of writing: the distinction between capital and lower-case letters. Tilgham noted:

> The Cathach of St Columba, dating perhaps from the early 7th century and possibly written by the saint himself, exemplifies one profoundly influential innovation of the Irish monks. To emphasize the beginning of an important passage, the scribes write its first letter much larger than the rest of the text and in a grander style. Slightly embarrassed by the difference in scale, they tend

to reduce each succeeding letter by a little until reaching the small scale of the ordinary text. Here, already, is the distinction between capitals and lower case (or in manuscript terms, majuscule and minuscule) which is later a standard feature of the western European script.[2]

Every book had to be laboriously copied by hand; there would be no printing press for another thousand years. Dark ink for lettering came from oak gall, a growth on oak trees caused by insects. In many cases, lettering done with this organic ink has lasted more than a thousand years without fading. Pens made of feathers from geese and other water birds were cut to a chisel point, then dipped in the ink. Some scribes in the late Classical period also used pens with copper tips.

A poem, allegedly by Saint Columba, describes the toil involved in hand-copying a manuscript. Note the types of colored inks used by the scribe:

My hand is weary with writing;
My sharp great point is not thick;

My slender-beaked pen juts forth
A beetle-hued draught of bright blue ink.

A steady stream of wisdom springs
From my well-coloured neat fair hand;
On the page it pours its draught of ink
Of the green-skinned holly.

I send my little dripping pen unceasingly
Over an assemblage of books of great beauty,
To enrich the possessions of artists—
Whence my hand is weary with writing.[3]

When we picture a medieval scribe, our mind conjures up the image of a male cleric, but women were also scribes in the Early Middle Ages. The Book of Chad, produced at the same time as the Book of Kells and the Lindisfarne Gospels, includes glosses revealing that women were involved in the scriptorium where it was produced (in Lichfield, England).[4] Three prayer books produced in Mercia around 800 also appear to have been manufactured by women, as their subject matter focuses on women, and historians note that their "language lapses subconsciously from the masculine to feminine voice."[5] French female orders in the following century were dedicated to the work of copying and illuminating sacred texts. There are no proven examples of female scribes in Ireland, but it seems likely that they existed, given that the monastery in Kildare was comprised of both men and women, and women were copyists in areas where the Irish had evangelized.

An Old English riddle from the year 709 describes the process of producing vellum and turning it into a book:

> An enemy ended my life, deprived me of my physical strength; then he dipped me in water and drew me out again, and put me in the sun where I soon shed all my hair. After that the knife's sharp edge bit into me and all my blemishes were scraped away; fingers folded me and the bird's feather often moved over my brown surface, sprinkling meaningful marks. It swallowed more wood-dye and again traveled over me leaving black tracks. Then a man bound me, he stretched skin over me and adorned me with gold; thus I am enriched by the wondrous work of smiths, wound about with shining metal. Who am I?[6]

The physical properties of ancient documents can also be particularly revealing when it comes to furthering our understanding of the past. The Faddan Mor Psalter, for example, dated to 800 and unearthed from an Irish peat bog in 2006, has leaves of Egyptian papyrus attached to its cover—giving us further proof of the close connection between Irish and Egyptian Coptic Christianity in the Early Middle Ages.[7]

The saying "You can't judge a book by its cover" seems to have been disregarded as much in the Middle Ages as it is now—if not more. Medieval Bible covers were elaborate, with rich decorations intended to do justice to the spiritual treasures contained within their binding. A good example is the eighth-century Stonyhurst Gospel of John, a Hiberno-Saxon illuminated manuscript, which is enclosed in a goatskin cover. Pieces of leather were molded over cord to produce the image of the Tree of Life' on the front cover—perhaps reminding readers that the contents of John's Gospel were like the tree of paradise, a sacrament offering eternal life. Although some Insular manuscripts are missing their covers, this attests to how richly the original covers were ornamented; Viking raiders sometimes tore pages of books out of their gilded and jeweled covers, discarded the pages, and kept the covers, since the precious metals held value for them that the vellum pages did not. For the Celtic Christians, however, hand-copied Scriptures were valuable indeed.

That did not prevent them from being well used. Some illuminated Bibles were large and heavy, intended for use as pulpit Bibles, but others were designed to be easily transportable. The Saint Cuthbert Gospel, the earliest existent book made in Europe, which was buried with its owner in 687, is a leather-bound copy of John's Gospel that measures only five by four inches. The Gospel of Saint Mulling in Trinity College Dublin and a comparable Irish volume in the British Library contain all four Gospels and are the same compact size. These works are outstanding examples of the scribal art, since it is more difficult to execute elegant script on a small scale, and the latter two examples include illuminated pages similar to larger Bible manuscripts.

Such so-called "pocket Gospels" were designed so that monks could transport them easily on their travels, for purposes of evangelism or pastoral care. The monks carried these small Bibles secured in leather satchels with shoulder straps. A carved stone from Burra, Shetland, combining Pagan and Christian motifs and possibly dating from the time of the evangelization of the Picts in Northern Scotland, portrays Christian monks, one of them wearing a book-sized satchel affixed by a strap over his neck. Perhaps this was how the Picts first beheld Christianity: meeting cowled monks who carried the written words of the Gospel in order to read aloud its life-changing words.[8]

Several saints' legends are illustrative of the Christian Celts' regard for the Scriptures. The first concerns Brigid, the saint who bridges Pagan and Christian traditions, and who is portrayed as the most Christ-like of Irish believers. Brigid's charioteer, Aed, tells her that he is sad, for he does not own a copy of the Gospels. Brigid asks Aed to pray with her for a copy of the Sacred Word, and then she reaches into her *sinus* (Latin for "lap" or "bosom") and draws out a copy of the Scriptures.[9] This story highlights the supernatural nature of the texts, their nurturing power, and the cherished nature of the Word. Brigid, the Mary of the Gaels, miraculously conceives the Word (which can be either "Christ" or "Scripture" in Christian symbolism) in the most intimate part of her body.

Two more stories of a saint and the Scriptures concern Columba of Iona:

> One day Baithéne came to St. Columba and said, "I need one of the brethren to help me go through the text of the psalter I have copied and correct any mistakes." The saint answered, "Why do you bring this trouble on us when there is no need? For in your copy of the psalter there is no mistake—neither one letter too many nor one too few—except that in one place the letter 'i' is missing." When they proofed the entire psalter, it was found to be exactly as the saint predicted.[10]

This tale demonstrates the scrupulous nature of copying the Scriptures. A second story of Columba reveals the great value attached to these manuscripts, and also the fact that a greatly esteemed abbot like Columba was not above doing the scribal work himself. In fact, copying sacred texts was one of the most important tasks for a leader in the Celtic church. Adomnán, Columba's hageographer, tells the story:

Once a book of the week's hymns written out by St. Columba with his own hand fell into the water when the boy who was carrying it in a leather satchel on his shoulders slipped off a bridge over a river in the province of Leinster. The book remained in the water from Christmas to Easter, until it was found on the riverbank by some women out walking. They took it to a priest named Éogenénan, a man of Pictish origin, to whom it had belonged. The book was still in its satchel, which was not merely sodden but had rotted. When Éogenénan opened the satchel, however, he found the book unharmed, as clean and dry as if it had never fallen into the water but had remained in its book case.[11]

A charming and less miraculous insight into scribal life is the famous poem about a scholar and his cat, Pangur Ban. The scribe, like many other writers, knew the quiet sense of companionship a cat can offer while both writer and cat goes about his own business.

I and Pangur Ban my cat,
'Tis a like task we are at:

Hunting mice is his delight,
Hunting words I sit all night.

Better far than praise of men
'Tis to sit with book and pen;
Pangur bears me no ill will,
He too plies his simple skill.

'Tis a merry thing to see
At our tasks how glad are we,
When at home we sit and find
Entertainment to our mind.

Oftentimes a mouse will stray
In the hero Pangur's way;
Oftentimes my keen thought set
Takes a meaning in its net.

'Gainst the wall he sets his eye
Full and fierce and sharp and sly;
'Gainst the wall of knowledge I
All my little wisdom try.

When a mouse darts from its den
O how glad is Pangur then!
O what gladness do I prove
When I solve the doubts I love!

So in peace our tasks we ply,
Pangur Ban, my cat, and I;
In our arts we find our bliss;
I have mine and he has his.

Practice every day has made
Pangur perfect in his trade;
I get wisdom day and night
Turning darkness into light.[12]

We may imagine the life of early-medieval scribes from a romantic perspective; don't we wish sometimes that we could swap out our stressful office job to become a monk sitting in the scriptorium happily scratching away for hours without the stresses of modern life? Yet daily life has never been easy. The end of a seventh-century commentary on Scripture, composed on Iona, says:

> Each day brings an almost insupportable amount of ecclesiastical demands from every side and I have had to write the book amidst many laborious preoccupations . . . so do not forget to pray . . . for me.[13]

By the eighth century, Celtic scribes had achieved extraordinary heights of artistry, so that illuminated manuscripts such as the Book of Kells and the Lindisfarne Gospels rank among the greatest works of calligraphy that have ever been produced. The Book of Chad and the Hereford Gospels indicate that Celtic scribes in Western England and Wales rivaled the skills of their brethren on the holy islands of Iona and Lindisfarne.

A look at the materials needed to produce the Book of Kells demonstrates the worth of these calligraphic masterpieces. Rare substances were imported for the colors: purple leaves from Italy and lapis lazuli for the blue coloring, possibly imported from the Himalaya Mountains of India.

Even more precious than the physical elements needed for its composition was the time, effort, and extraordinary artistic talent that went into the work. It is estimated that four or five scribes and artists working together would have needed about thirty years to finish a book.[14] Some elements of the calligraphy are so tiny that they rival the precision of marks on a dollar bill; they hardly seem possible if done by unaided eyes, and in fact a clue to their composition may reside in the Edinburgh National Museum—a magnifying lens taken from a medieval monastery. With the materials, effort, and artistic genius that went into making a masterpiece like the Book of Kells it is no wonder that Gerald of Wales in the twelfth century called it "the work not of men, but of angels."[15]

Even in the increasingly secular twenty-first century, exhibitions of the great Celtic Bible manuscripts draw crowds. Gazing at these works of genius, viewers should remember that for these early-medieval Christians, all their efforts to create visual splendor could only capture flashes of the majesty of God's written word and glimpses of the High King of Heaven's glory. For them, the worth of the Bible's message far exceeded the value of any physical representation.

It may be difficult for us, living in the twenty-first century, to feel the sense of excitement that the Celts had when reading the Bible. For them, all the stories were new and amazing, in every sense a revelation. We, on the other hand, see the Bible as something very old and—according to some people—outdated. The Bible has become fodder for today's polarizing cultural and political battles, so that when some folks hear proclaimed, "the Bible says," they feel a warm sense of comfort and authority, while others might hear "the Bible says" as a veiled sort of threat.

Perhaps we can recapture some of the Celts' enchantment with the Scriptures by gazing at the wondrous art of the Book of Kells and other scribal masterpieces. The Celtic monks worked hard to convey a sense of Divine Mystery in their work and that still shines across the ages. Sometimes, illumination from the ancient past can reveal the road ahead.

Notes

1. Benjamin C. Tilgham, "Writing in Tongues: Mixed Scripts and Style in Insular Art," in Colum Hourihane, *Insular & Anglo-Saxon Art & Thought in the Early Medieval Period* (Princeton, NJ: Princeton University Press, 2011), 93.

2. "History of Writing," History World, http://www.history-world.net/wrldhis/PlainTextHistories.asp?ParagraphID=-fle. [Accessed December 2, 2015.]

3. In Maureen O'Rourke Murphy and James MacKillop, editors, *An Irish Literature Reader: Poetry, Prose, Drama* (Syracuse, NY: Syracuse University Press, 2006), 25.

4. Linda Blackford, "University of Kentucky scholar hopes to uncover new clues about origin of 8th-century Gospels," *Lexington Herald-Leader,* July 3, 2014,

5. Michael W. Herren and Shirley Ann Brown, *Christ in Celtic Christianity: Britain and Ireland from the Fifth to the Tenth Century* (Woodbridge, Suffolk, UK: Boydell Press, 2012), 36.

6. George Otto Sims, *Exploring the Book of Kells* (Dublin: O'Brien Press, 2008), 27–28.

7. Jerome Reilly. "Manuscript Dug from Bog Rates Among Our Top 10 Biggest Finds," *Independent* Sept. 5, 2010, https://www.independent.ie/irish-news/manuscript-dug-from-bog-rates-among-our-top-10-biggest-finds-26678101.html. [Accessed April 10, 2019.]

8. This is my own reading of the Papil stone, from observing it first hand at the Edinburgh National Museum.

9. Joseph Falaky Nagy, *Conversing with Angels & Ancients: Literary Myths of Medieval Ireland* (Ithaca, NY: Cornell University Press, 1997), 237.

10. Adomnán of Iona, *Life of Saint Columba* (London: Penguin, 1995), 129–130.

11. Ibid., 161.

12. Maureen O'Rourke Murphy and James MacKillop, *Irish Literature: A Reader* (Syracuse, NY: Syracuse University Press, 1987), 22.

13. Thomas O'Loughlin, *Journeys on the Edges: The Celtic Tradition* (New York: Maryknoll, 2000), 134.

14. Simms, 65.

15. Giraldis Cambrensis (Gerard of Wales), *The History and Topography of Ireland,* ed. and trans. John O'Meara (New York: Penguin Books, 1982), 84.

PART 2

The Peacock's Feathers

Principles of Celtic Bible Interpretation

For there are many ways,
indeed an infinite number,
of interpreting the Scriptures,
just as in one and the same feather of a peacock
and even in the same small portion of the feather,
we see a marvelously beautiful variety
of innumerable colors.

—John Scottus Eriugena, *Periphyseon*, 866[1]

FOUR
Three Dimensions

Beautiful Variety

When a peacock's tail feathers are raised for courting, they transect the bird's body and form an extraordinary fan shape. The "eyes" seem to jump out from gauze-like feathers; they oscillate and sparkle with iridescent hues. The tapestry of shapes and colors changes constantly, depending on the peacock's motions, the angle of sunlight on the filaments of its tail, and the relative locations of the bird and viewer. This display of plumage is truly one of Nature's great marvels—and when Eriugena compared the Bible to a peacock's feathers, he was saying something about the Bible that many modern Christians might find quite radical.

John Scottus Eriugena, whose name translates as "John the Irishman from Ireland," has been described as a poet, mystic, philosopher, and theologian, one of the most accomplished thinkers of the Early Middle Ages.[2] Like many of his Gaelic brethren, Eriugena believed that the mystery and beauty of the Bible required the readers to look at each portion of Scripture from multiple perspectives. As readers view Scripture first from one angle and then from another, the written words of God reveal new, surprising, and life-giving truths. Like the splendor of the peacock's train, the beauty of Scripture is dynamic, ever-changing, catching light and meaning from its context that deepens and illuminates new hues and patterns.

This perspective does not in any way diminish the importance of Scripture. Yet the ways that the ancient Gaels interpreted Scripture differ markedly from the way that Christians today approach the same texts. This is an important lesson to bear in mind, since today those who love the

Bible *differently* are sometimes accused of not valuing the Bible at all. And perhaps the ancient multifold approach to Bible reading could be useful in our time, to fill up what may be lacking in our modern approach. Learning how our ancestors in the faith approached the words of God may offer us a chance to read more deeply.

Treasures from Afar

Once every three years the fleet of Tarshish came,
bringing gold, silver, ivory, apes, and peacocks.
—1 Kings 10:22 NASB

In Bible days, the peacock's mystique owed much to its exotic origins; it came from the faraway and fabled East. Centuries later, Europeans in the Middle Ages felt much the same about peacocks, as well as other imported wonders.

Living in the British Isles, the Celts were never far from the sea, and there was always the possibility that something strange and wonderful would arrive on a nearby shore: fabric, spices, foreign persons, or, best of all and as valuable to the Celts as gold, previously unknown knowledge. The Celtic scholar-saints coveted such foreign wisdom.

Those of us who live in the twenty-first century often value—and romanticize—Celtic Christianity for the ways it differs from other forms of faith. Celtic saints are portrayed as dreamy-eyed mystics, living in a magical world beyond the fringes of the Roman Empire. In reality, Celtic Christians did differ from their neighbors in some ways, but their commonalities with the rest of the Christian world outweighed their differences. As modern Christians, we often forget that medieval Christianity as a whole looked at the world, Scripture, and even God in ways that may seem strange to some of us today.

Celtic scholars were familiar with the medieval world's great Bible interpreters. Although they had their own theologians, the great African theologian Augustine of Hippo also influenced their thinking.[3] Enthralled by the tales of the Desert Fathers and Mothers, the Gaels devoured the saints' lives written by Anthony, Paul of Thebes, and others. The Celts were also conversant with the writers and thinkers of the Egyptian Church, including Origen. Enamored with monastic life, the Celts eagerly read the writings of John Cassian, who brought the Desert monastic way from Palestine to nearby France.[4] They also delighted in Jerome's work, which he conducted in Bethlehem (with the help of two female scholars), translating the Hebrew and Greek texts into Latin.

Syrians may also have influenced the Celtic Church. Columbanus relates how, when he was in Europe, a Syrian woman gave him food in an emergency, telling him, "I am a stranger like yourself, and come from the distant sun of the East." Albert Cook of Yale, regarded as one of the greatest philologists of the late nineteenth and early centuries, said, "In Gaul, Syrian and Eastern monasticism was flourishing when Christianity passed over to Ireland. In Irish monasticism we should therefore expect to find traces of Syrian and Oriental practices."[5] Syrian influence is particularly intriguing, insofar as the early Syriac churches were strongly influenced by their Jewish neighbors, and students of Celtic Christianity have noted how practices of the Celtic churches reflect those of Judaism.

Treasures from the Celtic World

While learning from civilizations around the world, the Celts also valued the contributions of their own local authors. Pelagius is sometimes considered the earliest representative of a distinctly Celtic Christian faith. This fifth-century Welshman often butted heads theologically with Augustine of Hippo. Pelagius emphasized free will and the pursuit of moral perfection in Christian life, while Augustine placed greater weight on Divine election and salvation by God's grace alone. Augustine prevailed outside of the Celtic realms, but Pelagius' influence continued in Gaelic lands. A survey of citations by Irish scribes found Augustine quoted eleven times, Origen twenty-one times, Jerome one hundred and sixteen—and Pelagius quoted 1,316 times.[6] Apparently, when Imperial authorities declared Pelagius a heretic, the Celts refused to read the memo!

The Celtic Christians of the Early Middle Ages worked hard to mine all the riches of Scripture, employing multiple dimensions of interpretation. But before we look at their techniques, we might ask how these ancient methods of Bible study have been preserved. Where can we find their understandings? Modern scholars know Gaelic Bible interpretations of the Early Middle ages via three types of written works: glosses, commentaries, and homilies.

Glosses are written comments added by readers to the margins of existent texts, much as modern readers might write notes in the borders and highlight favorite passages in a book. Glosses are common in ancient Celtic copies of the Psalms and Gospels, and also in less sacred books. Sometimes, a single text might have multiple glosses, added by successive readers. More than 12,000 of these marginal writings have survived, most of them written in the Irish language. (Not all of the notations are spiritual or theological in nature; for example, one anonymous ninth-century scribe scrawled in the Ogham alphabet, "Ale is killing us," a confession that may have indicated he was suffering from a nasty hangover.[7])

The Celts also wrote books of formal commentary on the Bible that were meant to be read in tandem with the Scriptures themselves. The tradition of Celtic Bible commentary began early in the fourth century, when the first Celtic theologian, Morgan of Wales (also known as Pelagius), wrote his commentaries on the Pauline Epistles. Another commentary, *On the Miracles of Holy Scripture*, written by an Irishman in the year 655, touches on numerous biblical texts spanning from Genesis to the Acts of the Apostles.[8] Others, such as Cummian's commentary on Mark and Eriugena's commentary on John, are specific to a certain book of the Bible.

In addition to glossalia and commentaries, modern scholars have ancient Celtic sermon notes. Love for the Bible coupled with the Celts' bardic talents produced exceptional sermons, and we are fortunate that many were written down. These homilies are particularly useful in understanding how biblical themes were used to address everyday concerns.

Added together, these glosses, commentaries, and sermon notes enable us to see the ways that Gaelic Christians interpreted the Bible. We can then divide Celtic Bible interpretation into three broad categories, or methods of interpretation—reading in three dimensions, as it were, with each dimension revealing different shades of meaning, all part of the same iridescent fan of light and truth. Some interpreters saw three levels of meaning in the text, others saw four, but many medieval theologians favored the threefold approach because it corresponded to the triune nature of humanity: body, mind, and soul.

It seems to me that each of the three dimensions can be likened to an aspect of the peacock's plumage. The first way of reading the Bible is the "grounded" or literal approach, corresponding to the physical structure of a peacock feather. The second way of reading the Bible is on the level of symbolism, equivalent to the manner in which the human eye perceives patterns in peacock plumage. The third way of Bible reading is that of imagination, likened to the way these birds have inspired artists to create new and dazzling visions. Each of the three dimensions is valuable: this approach is "both-and" rather than "either-or." Quoting Ecclesiastes, "a threefold cord is not quickly broken" (4:12).[9]

Practicing the Celtic Way

In the following sections we'll look at each of these three dimensions of interpretation. Each section will begin with ancient examples, followed by a consideration of the abiding relevance of the principle under discussion, and conclude with an example of how we might examine a Scripture passage from that perspective.

We should remember, as we read and practice these methods of interpretation, that the Celts did not ponder the Bible as isolated individuals (the rare exceptions being occasional hermits) but in community. Three forms of communal information-sharing are apparent. First, since monasteries were the backbone of Celtic spirituality, almost all Bible interpretation was conducted in a context of shared spiritual life. Second, there was exchange of information—books, letters, and envoys—throughout the world where the faith had spread. The seaways could be used like the Internet is used today, linking thinkers spatially distant from one another. Finally, there was an exchange of ideas over time. Since all books were hand-copied, they were highly prized and carefully handled, so many lasted for centuries. As Bible texts were passed down over long years, different readers in succession wrote glosses in the margins, sometimes in response to the glosses written by their predecessors. These comments beside the texts therefore became a sort of conversation across time, a precious compilation of different readers' wisdom.

In the New Testament Epistles, the word "you" is usually plural (a fact we miss, since only the American South's "y'all" offers an English-language version of the second-person plural pronoun that exists in many other languages). The ancient Celts provide a healthy model of reading the Bible with "you-all," a community of individuals in vital and intimate relationship with one another, across both time and space.

Notes

1. John Scottus Eriugena, *Periphyseon on the Division of Nature*, trans. I. P. Sheldon-Williams (Washington, DC: Dumbarton-Oaks, 1987), 390.

2. Dirdre Carabine, *John Scottus Eriugena* (New York: Oxford University Press, 2000), 13.

3. Thomas O'Loughlin, *Celtic Theology: Humanity, World and God in Early Irish Writings* (London: Continuum, 2005), 78. O'Loughlin indicates that Adomnán wrote *De Loci Sanctis* as a response to Augustine's call for such a book.

4. Ibid., 53.

5. Albert S. Cook, "The Name Caedmon," in *Publications of the Modern Language Association of America* VI, 1891: 16.

6. Leslie Hardinge, *The Celtic Church in Britain* (New York: Teach Services, 2005), 16.

7. Anglandicus, "Massive Scribal Hangovers: One Ninth Century Confession," December 7, 2014, http://anglandicus.blogspot.com/2014/12/massive-scribal-hangovers-one-ninth.html. [Accessed December 11, 2019.]

8. John Carey, *King of Mysteries: Early Irish Religious Writings* (Dublin: Four Courts Press, 2000), 51–74.

9. The term "three-dimensional" make sense to our modern minds, but it is anachronistic to the early Christian Celts. (It was first used in 1872, according to the *Merriam-Webster's Collegiate Dictionary*). Hardinge (*The Celtic Church in Britain*, 18) describes a threefold division with ancient Irish and Latin terms distinguishing *stoir* (as in storehouse, referring to the literal sense of the text), *sens* (allegory), and *run* (the "hidden" or mystical meaning). This choice of three divisions can be compared with Origen's interpretive schema that was widely circulated throughout the world in the late Classical Era and the Early Middle Ages. Corresponding to the three elements of human beings (body, soul, and spirit), Origen postulated three layers of meaning in each biblical text (literal, moral, and spiritual). For Origen's three-part division, see Karlfried Froehlich, *Biblical Interpretation in the Early Church* (Philadelphia: Fortress Press, 1984), 17. Origen's three-level interpretive scheme was expanded in the Middle Ages into a "four-senses" approach (literal, moral, allegorical, and anagogical). For the fourfold scheme, see "Hermeneutics" in the online *Encyclopedia Britannica* at https://www.britannica.com/topic/hermeneutics-principles-of-biblical-interpretation. [Accessed March 19, 2019.] I choose not to follow the exact terms of any of the ancient interpretive divisions, believing that the threefold division of literal, symbolic, and imaginative perspectives fits better with modern constructs of reality—hence my own "three-dimensional" approach. This model does, however, correspond loosely with the three ancient terms listed by Hardinge.

FIVE

The First Dimension

Grounded in Physical Reality

Reason herself . . . if we could but listen to her more carefully, insists that we should understand the relation which exists between the sacred texts and reality.

—Eriugena, *Periphyseon*

Gazing at a peacock shaking its fanned tail feathers, viewers are mesmerized by the way light catches and reveals shifting and shimmering iridescent colors. But few who fix their eyes on this astonishing spectrum realize the cause of the peacock's changing hues: microscopic crystal-like structures within the vanes of each feather reflect different properties of light, depending on how they are spaced. If it weren't for this complex physical arrangement, the peacock would not be so stunning.

In a similar way, the peacock-like diversity of meaning in Scripture depends upon correspondence with physical reality. The first dimension of Celtic Bible interpretation, the physical grounding of each passage,[1] begins with consideration of the ways its message is set within space and time.

This approach to understanding the Bible seems common sense to most modern readers; in fact, for many today it is the only way they know to read Scripture. "Focus on the *ad litteram* sense," writes biblical scholar Michael Graves in *The Inspiration and Interpretation of Scripture*, "is what most distinctively characterizes modern Biblical studies, both in the academy and in the church."[2]

Yet this has not always been the case. For long periods of church history, symbolic interpretations were regarded as more important than the literal meanings. Origen, one of the most dedicated and influential scholars of the Bible in early church history, wrote:

> The Scriptures were composed through the spirit of God and they have not only that meaning which is obvious, but also another which is hidden from the majority of readers. For the contents of Scripture are the outward forms of certain mysteries and the images of divine things.[3]

Eucherius, founder of the monastic center at Lerins, France, who had a significant impact on Irish Christianity, also emphasized the multiple levels of meaning in the Bible. He encouraged readers to "see through the surface [historical] level of Scripture to its 'higher' spiritual meaning."[4]

While the great scholars of the wider world encouraged the Gaels to seek out the higher symbolic meanings of the Bible, one of their own teachers emphasized the literal sense. The Welshman Pelagius was a brilliant Bible scholar whose commentaries contain very little symbolic interpretation; in fact, his expositions of Scripture read much like modern Evangelical commentaries. Pelagius emphasized human capacity to choose for-or-against God, a potential he believed was implanted in each individual as bearers of God's image (Genesis 1:26). God bestows knowledge leading to salvation, said Pelagius, and the Bible is the foremost revelation of the Divine will. For this reason, Pelagius focused on legal and didactic texts (as opposed to stories) in the Bible, and he explained these commandments in their most literal sense. "Pelagians trusted a virtuous ascetic to read and interpret the Scriptures for him- or herself," write historians Michael W. Herren and Shirley Ann Brown, "believing it was better to trust the reader's own interpretation than to absorb a commentary author's 'false allegorisation of the law.'"[5] Although Christians outside the British Isles deemed Pelagius a heretic, his writings held sway over the Celtic saints for four hundred years, and therefore his literal interpretations of the Bible counterbalanced the more symbolic readings that were also an aspect of the Celts' understanding of the Bible.

Celtic Christianity is pervaded by a sense that the sacred is grounded in the natural world. This meant that for the Celts, there were two books of God available for human interpretation—the Book of God written in ink on vellum, and the vastly larger Book of God that comprised all of Creation.[6] Since God expressed God's Self through the medium of the material world, the Celts had to be open to the grounded interpretation of the Scriptures, as well as the symbolic.

In the seventh century, a scholar known as the "Irish Augustine" wrote a commentary titled *On the Miracles of Scripture*, which reveals a peculiarly Hibernian grounded perspective.[7] This commentary sets out to provide "natural" explanations for all the miracles in the Bible.[8] The Irish Augustine reads the whole Bible from the firmly grounded perspective that "all of God's acts . . . must have been accomplished in accordance with nature and not in contravention of its laws."[9] If this treatise on miracles had been written in the modern era, readers would consider it a "scientific" approach to the Bible's wonders.

One striking example of the Irish Augustine's approach is the section "On the Incarnation of Our Lord Jesus Christ, and his birth from the Virgin Mary." Contemplating what many Christians would consider the superlative miracle in all history, the Irish Augustine claims that the Virgin Birth was a natural event. "Although it is indeed contrary to all of human experience for conception to be accomplished without a man's seed, it was not outside of nature" because "we can point to . . . animals generated without the intercourse of parents . . . birds and . . . many fish."[10] In our time, biologists confirm these examples of parthenogenesis in Nature. The Irish Augustine was both a keen observer of the natural world, and an ingenious interpreter of Scripture, qualities reflecting the Celtic allegiance to God's revelation in both "books" of God—the Bible and the environment.

The Continuing Relevance of the Celts' Grounded Interpretation

Reading the Bible as grounded in time and space is a practice with perennial value because God has addressed humanity through the medium of the physical world. The Bible has specific historical and geographical contexts, and to ignore those is to risk misinterpreting the intended meanings. Since scriptures are rooted in history, the Bible should—to a significant degree—be read in light of its physical origins.[11]

Although at first glance the Celtic grounded approach resembles the method of Bible study employed by most Christians today, it differs from contemporary literalism in two regards. First, this grounded reading was balanced by symbolic and imaginative insights. Second, the Celts' reading—unlike that often employed in American Evangelical circles—regarded the letter of the biblical text as a voice, but *not the only voice*, of God's utterance.

For the past five centuries, Protestant Bible scholarship has been strongly influenced by the Reformer's motto "*Sola Scriptura*."[12] In its more restrictive sense, this means that the Bible is regarded as the supreme authority in all matters of Christian doctrine and practice. In some literalist churches, that doctrine is expanded to assert the Bible's overruling authority in all fields of human knowledge, including science, economics, health, and politics.

This totalizing of the Bible makes sense to many modern-day Christians, but other believers find it difficult to swallow. Bible scholar Peter Enns confesses, "The Bible can become a challenge to one's faith in God rather than the source of faith, a problem to be overcome rather than the answer to our problems."[13] This troubling-of-faith is apparent in the lives of college students reared in literalist homes and then exposed to scientific knowledge. Many American Evangelicals deny Evolution (due to its contradiction with a literalist reading of Genesis 1) and deny climate change (based on a literalist reading of Genesis 8:22).[14] That can lead to painful struggles between what students have been told is Bible truth and the realities of the physical world—but this unfortunate collision is not inevitable. "The problem," as Peter Enns says, "is coming to the Bible with expectations it's not set up to bear."[15]

Celtic Christians in the Early Middle Ages understood Scripture and the world in a way that would have avoided this conflict. Since God's revelation is transmitted to humans both in the Bible *and* in the physical universe, the Bible need not be regarded as the sole repository of all human knowledge. They believed that while there are truths revealed in Scripture, there are also innumerable further truths coming to light as God speaks through the natural environment.

The Celtic grounded reading of the Bible has the potential to transform an authoritarian form of interpretation into one that's more open to exchange of ideas. For some modern Christians, when the Bible appears to contradict observations of the natural world, the Bible trumps reality. But in the Celtic understanding, God speaks in stereo—both through the Scriptures and through gains in human knowledge. Perceived differences between God's "two books" can be welcomed as occasions for dialogue between the two forms of revelation, with the possibility that gains in scientific knowledge will necessitate revised interpretations of the Scriptures. Such revisions are not "giving in to science" or compromising the Bible—they are blessed opportunities to view the peacock's beauty in a new way.

An Example of Grounded Bible Reading: Mark 10:46–52 WEB

We will use the passage that follows as an example of how to use each of the three different approaches to biblical interpretation. As you read the next chapters, you may wish to refer back again to this passage before you read about its meanings from a metaphorical and then an imaginative approach.

They came to Jericho. As he went out from Jericho, with his disciples and a great multitude, the son of Timaeus, Bartimaeus, a blind beggar, was sitting by the road. When he heard that it was Jesus the Nazarene, he began to cry out, and say, "Jesus, you son of David, have mercy on me!" Many rebuked him, that he should be quiet, but he cried out much more, "You son of David, have mercy on me!"

Jesus stood still, and said, "Call him."

They called the blind man, saying to him, "Cheer up! Get up. He is calling you!"

He, casting away his cloak, sprang up, and came to Jesus.

Jesus asked him, "What do you want me to do for you?"

The blind man said to him, "Rabboni, that I may see again."

Jesus said to him, "Go your way. Your faith has made you well." Immediately he received his sight, and followed Jesus on the way.

Reading this from a grounded perspective, we might begin by asking what we can know about the physical condition of blindness, particularly in the Ancient Middle East. Biblehub.com, a popular Bible study website, provides this information:

> This distressing malady is very prevalent in the East. Many physical causes in those countries unite to injure

> the organs of vision. The sun is hot, and in the atmosphere floats a very fine dust, which enters and frets the eye.

More specifically, "Blindness from birth is the result of a form of this disease known as *ophthalmia neonatorum* which sets in a few days after birth. Sometimes ophthalmia accompanies malarial fever."[16]

Following the example of the Irish Augustine in his work *On the Miracles of Scripture*, we might ask, "Can this healing can be explained in terms of natural law?" It could in fact be a case of psychosomatic blindness, such as that experienced by "that blind, deaf, and dumb boy" Tommy, in the Who rock opera. If psychological trauma caused Bartimaeus to go blind, then the overwhelming psychological power of Christ's verbal blessing might have cured him.

If the blindness was the sort of physical malady noted in the quotes above, then there was no medical cure existent at the time. Interpreters open to a more supernatural healing might enumerate which parts of the optical lens or neural organs of the eye might have been damaged, and how Jesus was able to miraculously perform by mere touch an operation surpassing what can be done by all the best technology of our age.

In the following sections, we'll see how adding levels of interpretation multiplies the ways this same text can be understood and applied to life.

Notes

1. I refer to "grounding" rather than "literal" for several reasons. I believe that this level of interpretation as practiced in the Insular Early Middle Ages is only very roughly similar to modern literalism (as I explain later in the chapter). "Grounded" holds the sense that it is the level of interpretation tied most closely to the surface of reality, the meanings pertaining to the visible world as opposed to a deeper, more mystical reading. The word "grounded" also refers to the Earth itself, and the connection with the organic world rooted in the soil of our planet is indicated in this approach. Finally, Bible narratives are "grounded" in the sense that they are "tied down" or "anchored" to their origins in space-and time.

2. Michael Graves, *The Inspiration and Interpretation of Scripture: What the Early Church Can Teach Us* (Grand Rapids, MI: Eerdmans, 2014), Kindle edition, location 2890.

3. Ibid., Kindle location 1091.

4. Thomas O'Loughlin, *Journeys on the Edges: The Celtic Tradition* (New York: Maryknoll, 2000), 39.

5. Michael W. Herren and Shirley Ann Brown, *Christ in Celtic Christianity: Britain and Ireland from the Fifth to the Tenth Century* (Woodbridge, Suffolk, UK: Boydell Press, 2012), 119.

6. Ibid., 35.

7. The name "Irish Augustine" comes from the fact that the work was erroneously believed for a time to be the work of Augustine of Hippo.

8. John Carey, *King of Mysteries: Early Irish Religious Writings* (Dublin: Colour Books, 2000), 51.

9. Ibid.

10. Ibid., 63.

11. Since many of the Bible texts have been substantially rewritten, collated, or redacted, we might do well to also add these redactors to this statement regarding writers.

12. In the Late Middle Ages, the Christian church was wracked by schism and scandal. The Protestant Reformers, seeking to restore the church to its purity, defied the Pope and separated from the leadership of the Roman church, creating the need for a new locus of authority. Scripture fulfilled that role, but doing so required the gradual reformulation of the Bible and its authority, first in the form of *Sola Scriptura* and later the doctrine of infallibility. Even the Catholic

Church was influenced by the Protestants' doctrine insofar as the Counter-Reformation reformulated Catholic doctrine as reaction to the Reformers.

13. Peter Enns, *The Bible Tells Me So: Why Defending Scripture Has Made Us Unable to Read It* (New York: HarperCollins, 2014), 6.

14. Around four in ten white evangelical Protestants (38%) say humans have always existed in their present form, and about a quarter (27%) of black Protestants share this view, according to a 2019 Pew study. Among white mainline Protestants, just 16 percent say humans have always existed in their present form. Similar shares of Catholics (13%) and the religiously unaffiliated (11%) say the same. Only among the religiously unaffiliated—those who describe their religion as atheist, agnostic or "nothing in particular"—do a majority (64%) accept Evolution via natural selection with no involvement from God or a higher power. (David Masci, "For Darwin Day, 6 Facts About the Evolution Debate," February 11, 2019, https://www.pewresearch.org/fact-tank/2019/02/11/darwin-day/ [accessed April 10, 2019]). A 2018 ABC poll suggests that while 66 percent of Americans think global warming is real and caused by human beings, only 32 percent of white Evangelicals do (Mark Silk, "A Religious Opening for Stopping Climate Change," *ANS Religious News Service*, November 29, 2018, https://religionnews.com/2018/11/29/a-religious-opening-for-climate-change/. [Accessed April 10, 2019].

15. Enns, 8.

16. "Blindness," Bible Hub, http://biblehub.com/topical/b/blindness.htm. [Accessed Nov. 26, 2015.]

SIX

The Second Dimension

Ascending to the Level of Symbolism

And this variety of interpretation
is not contrary to nature.

—Eriugena, *Periphyseon*

The beauty of the peacock's train lies not just in the variety of shimmering colors, but also in the pattern displayed by the outstretched fan. The first things you notice are the "eyes," ovals within ovals that jump out from the background color. Next, you may discern the arrangement of these "eyes" within the entire train; viewed together, they form a fractal design in which replication of smaller elements produces a larger pattern. No wonder that Hindus, Buddhists, Jews, Christians, and Muslims have all interpreted the peacock as having mystical significance. The beauty and complexity of its plumage beckons us to contemplate the splendor and mystery of a larger reality.

Contemplating the prevalence and complexity of designs in Nature, Augustine of Hippo (354–430) formulated a "sacramental vision of reality." In this view, "in even the least interesting bit of matter, there is a link to God."[1] This sacramental view of reality was inspired by Scripture itself: "For the invisible things of God since the creation of the world are clearly seen, being perceived through the things that are made" (Romans 1:20 WEB).

Eucherius of Gaul (380–449) likened the Bible to Nature: both are multidimensional forms of revelation. He wrote a book titled *Formula for a Spiritual Understanding,* influential in the Irish medieval monasteries, in which he invited readers past the purely historical meaning of Scripture into deeper, more spiritual meanings, based upon the Bible itself.

Listing elements of the natural world referred to in Scripture, such as the sun, moon, trees, fire, stones, and animals, he then pointed out other scriptural examples where that same object was used in a clearly metaphorical way. Eucherius discerned that throughout the Bible "there was the text you could read on the page in front of you, and there was the more real, more permanent and higher meaning to which it pointed through its symbolic codes."[2]

Such a metaphorical reading of Scripture is indeed pervasive in the Bible. The Apostle Paul, for example, was fond of symbolic interpretation, as he makes clear in his writing in the New Testament. In 1 Corinthians 10:4, he refers to the rock that Moses struck in Sinai and then says, "they drank from the spiritual rock that accompanied them, and that rock was Christ." In Galatians chapter 4, Paul refers to Abraham's two sons by two mothers and then later declares, "These things contain an allegory, for these are two covenants" (Galatians 10:24).[3] In these examples, Paul illustrates the kind of interpretation that would become common in the Early Middle Ages, seeing through the historical level of the Hebrew Bible to discern a higher spiritual meaning that speaks of Christ. No wonder then that "virtually all ancient

Christians believed that the Old Testament had spiritual meaning beyond the literal sense."[4]

Some early Christians had another pressing reason to adopt this method of interpretation: they were trying to preserve the Hebrew scriptures as being suitable for Christianity. Not all Christians agreed that these older scriptures still had value in the post-Incarnation world. Marcion (85–160), a Christian living in what is today Turkey, noted that the "Old Testament God" did things that seem unworthy of the God revealed in Christ. Could a God who demanded genocide of unbelievers (1 Samuel 15) be the same as a God who loves the world (John 3:16) and is love (John 4:8)? Could the same Divine Spirit command, "Do not leave alive anything that breathes" (Deuteronomy 20:16) and then speak through Jesus' lips saying "Love your enemies" (Matthew 5:44)? Marcion had a simple answer: do away with the Old Testament.

Origen (184–254), a Christian scholar living in Alexandria, Egypt, agreed with Marcion on one crucial point: "some Old Testament portrayals of God are unworthy of God."[5] Yet Origen's life was devoted to study of the Hebrew scriptures, which he treasured. As Eric Seibert writes in *Disturbing Divine Behavior*:

> Origen retained the Old Testament and sought to interpret it in such a way as to exclude from its depiction of God the qualities Marcion condemned. Marcion denied the validity of allegory. Origen spent his life employing allegory and seeking to justify the method.[6]

Origen defended Christian use of the Hebrew scriptures by interpreting the genocide passages symbolically. The Christian should read commands to slay pagans, Origen said, as symbolic calls to eradicate sin and disobedience. He wrote:

> If the horrible wars related in the Old Testament were not to be interpreted in a spiritual sense, the apostles would never have transmitted the Jewish books for reading in the church to followers of Christ.[7]

A century later, Augustine also used symbolic interpretation to deal with troubling Old Testament passages. How could a God of love possibly call for smashing the heads of Babylonian infants (Psalm 137:9)? According to Bible scholar Kenton L. Sparks, Augustine interpreted that verse as follows: "the 'infants' of Babylon were not literal children but rather the vices of the Babylonians."[8]

A scribe on the Scottish Island of Iona copying the famous Book of Kells around the year 800 seems to have had similar concerns regarding violent texts of the Bible. Matthew 10:34 usually says, "*I have come not to bring peace but a sword*" (NRSV), but in the Book of Kells it says, "*I came not to send peace, but joy.*" Professor Ian Bradley remarks, "Maybe this was a mistake, but it is tempting to suggest that he made the alteration because of his unease with the notion of Jesus as sword bearer."[9]

As a Celtic example of figurative reading, the earliest surviving commentary on the Gospel of Mark, written in 610 by the Irish monk Cummian, offers numerous examples of symbolic interpretation. Referring to the mistreatment of Jesus by the Sanhedrin (Mark 14:65), Cummian offers these observations:

> This was so that by his guilt he might remove our guilt; that by the blindfold on his face he might take the blindfold from our hearts; that by receiving the spits, he might wash the face of our soul, that by the blows, by which

> he was struck on the head, he might heal the head of the human race, which is Adam.[10]

These insights flow from Cummian's knowledge of other Scriptures, and his theological emphasis on the Gospel as the outworking of God's mercy. His broader knowledge led him to see God's kindness even in a series of horrible events.

As another example of Celtic symbolic interpretation, Aleran the Wise of County Meath, Ireland, wrote a book in 664 titled *The Mystical Interpretation of the Genealogy of Our Lord Jesus Christ*, in which he went through the genealogy of Christ that introduces Matthew's Gospel and gives a symbolic meaning for each name listed. For example, one ancestor of Christ was Obed, whose name means "servant" in Hebrew, and Aleran commented:

> Christ came not to be served but to serve, even taking on the form of a servant. . . . The Christian likewise may serve the Lord with that servitude which is not out of fear, but with the spirit of the adoption of sons.[11]

The Continuing Relevance of the Celts' Symbolic Interpretation

Interpreters in the modern era, part of a larger trend that favors didactic language over imaginative wording, have been dismissive of symbolic understanding of the Bible. In modernity, "The one who speaks powerfully is not the poet," wrote George Aichele in *Sign, Text and Scripture*, "but the scientist or engineer, who uses words to represent or manipulate the world."[12] Yet some of the greatest thinkers of our age have championed the importance of symbolism.

Huston Smith, a well-known Christian scholar of comparative religions, wrote:

> *Exegesis that stops with the literal meaning of a text . . . cannot do the text full justice.* Classical Christianity took it for granted that literalism could not do the full job, which is why "Jesus spoke to them in parables."

Smith concluded: "Religion's technical language is symbolism, the science of relations between the multiple levels of reality."[13]

C. S. Lewis, the twentieth-century grand spokesman of Christianity, asserted that

> allegory belongs to "the very nature of thought and language." It is a fragment of the perennial language, signaling immaterial feelings by material images that remain constant across the ages and around the world.[14]

Lewis dedicated several chapters to the importance of symbolic interpretation in his book *Reflections on the Psalms.* He wrote that since "pagan utterances can carry a second meaning . . . we shall expect the Scriptures to do this more momentously and more often."[15] Following in the tradition of Saint Augustine, Lewis addressed Psalm 137 as a text that benefits from symbolic reading.

> From this point of view I can use even the horrible passage in 137 about dashing the Babylonian babies against the stones. I know things in the inner world which are like babies; the infantile beginning of small indulgences, small resentments, which may one day become dipsomania or settled hatred . . . against

> all such petty infant . . . the advice of the Psalms is best.[16]

Marcus Borg, one of the twenty-first century's most insightful Jesus scholars, was also a defender of symbolic Bible interpretation. He called metaphor "the *more-than-literal meaning* of language" and affirmed that "there is more than one justification for using a metaphorical approach to the Bible. One reason is that much of its language is obviously metaphorical . . . even when a text contains historical memory, its more-than-literal meaning matters most. For example, the exile in Babylon in the sixth century BCE really happened, but the way the story is told gives it a more-than-historical meaning. It became a metaphorical narrative of exile and return, abiding images of the human condition and its remedy."[17]

In another book, Borg emphasized that "metaphor is about surplus of meaning, not a deficiency of meaning." The Gospel accounts, Borg believed, include "*memory metaphorized*—stories that contain the memory of something that happened, but that are told in such a way as to give them a more than historical-factual meaning." An example is Mark's account of Jesus' journey to Jerusalem leading to his sacrificial death. Borg explained:

> Jesus really did make a journey from Galilee to Jerusalem that ended in his execution. This is history remembered. But the way Mark tells the story of Jesus' journey gives it a more-than-historical meaning. In Mark it is a story of *what it means to follow Jesus* . . . for Mark (and early Christianity generally), to be a *disciple* is to *follow* Jesus on *the way* to Jerusalem . . . to follow Jesus is to join him on this journey of transformation and confrontation. The story of Jesus' final journey is a metaphorical narrative about the meaning of discipleship.[18]

Following a similar train of thought, Wheaton College biblical studies professor Michael Graves wrote:

> If Scripture is to speak credibly to contemporary Christians, the exposition of Scripture must move beyond recounting the *ad litteram* sense. . . . Therefore, although it is often not obvious to modern Christians, we have much to learn from the Church Fa-

thers about how to interpret Scripture beyond the literal level.[19]

There is another factor that highlights the contemporary importance of symbolic interpretation. The Bible is critiqued today for the same reason that it was questioned in the second century—the perilous shadow of its violent passages. At a time when the world is reeling from religious terrorism, Christ's followers hesitate to add fuel to an already destructive conflagration.

Philip Jenkins, Distinguished Senior Fellow at the Institute for Studies of Religion at Baylor University, questions whether the Quran endorses violence more than the Bible—and answers in the negative: "If the founding text shapes the whole religion, then Judaism and Christianity deserve the utmost condemnation as religions of savagery." He goes on, however, to note, "Of course, they are no such thing; nor is Islam."[20] As Jenkins points out, Abrahamic religions each have scriptures that can be used to promote violence or peace, and if they are to result in peace, then the teachers of religion must learn to talk about violent passages constructively. Jenkins reminds us that in the accounts of Old Testament genocide,

> we have a constructed narrative in which particular authors and editors have taken a story and framed it in ways that made sense to them. It is a story with a point or theme, and one that is aimed at a particular audience.[21]

Investigating the conquest of Canaan, archaeologists find evidence that differs from the Bible tales. According to Jenkins, "Archaeologist William Dever concludes that . . . evidence 'supports almost nothing of the biblical account of a large scale concerted Israelite military invasion of Canaan.'"[22] So why would the Bible writers exaggerate tales of how they exterminated their enemies right down to the noncombatants? The answer may be that the Bible was mostly written after the Babylonian exile, a time at which Jews were wondering: how can we make sure history does not repeat for us? To ensure Israel's future purity, the Bible writers portrayed a golden age of Israel, before they fell into God's disfavor. This golden age was marked by absolute loyalty to God's commandments. The wars in Canaan were portrayed as the utter extermination of everything that did not faithfully worship God, as an illustration of the way that faithful Israel should expunge everything ungodly from their midst. The Bible stories of genocide may have been composed to point to a larger truth—the need to utterly eradicate idolatry—rather than a straightforward recounting of history. Thus, the best current scholarship supports the instincts of the ancient interpreters: in a culture of literary traditions quite different from ours today, biblical tales of violence were intended to be understood for their spiritual meaning rather than taken as literal history.

Professor Michael concurs, saying,

> The Philistines are typologized in the Old Testament as the ultimate "other" in a manner that, even if it reflects historical realities to some extent, also places a theological overlay on top of history. The Church Fathers' belief in a higher sense gave them a framework within which to perceive such theological overlays. For reasons such as these, the interpretations that the Church Fathers identified as the spiritual sense sometimes correlate with ideas genuinely found in the biblical texts.[23]

So there are compelling reasons—both the symbolic nature of many Bible passages and the continuing need to properly interpret violent passages—that commend the "more-than-literal" reading of Scripture. But some church historians allege that the Middle Ages were the Dark Ages in terms of Bible reading. Allegorical analysis of the Bible led to a profusion of ridiculous and unmerited interpretations. If today's Christians again embrace the symbolic nature of Scripture, will that lead to confusion?

This question wrongly supposes, however, that the literal meaning is always more easily understood than the symbolic meaning. In fact, the "clear and simple" meaning of the Bible is often the product of a group's or an individual's bias. As Graves has observed, "Many modern teachers of Scripture arbitrarily devise their own (sometimes idiosyncratic) applications of biblical texts and impose them on others as if with divine authority."[24] Similarly, Bible scholar N. T. Wright noted:

> We imagine that we are "reading the text straight," and that if somebody disagrees with us it must be because they, unlike ourselves, are secretly using "presuppositions" of this or that sort. This is simply naive, and actually astonishingly arrogant and dangerous. . . . Evangeli-

cals often use the phrase "authority of scripture" when they *mean* the authority of evangelical or Protestant theology, since the assumption is made that we (Evangelicals or Protestants) are the ones who know and believe what the Bible is saying.[25]

An illustration may serve to show the problem of discerning a "clear" literal meaning. I've often heard Christians say something along these lines: "The Bible does not command slavery—God never desired human bondage." I am thankful they read Scripture that way, but this was not always the "clear" meaning of the Bible. In fact, a vast array of Bible tracts, sermons, and theological arguments before America's Civil War cited chapter and verse to support the viewpoint that the simple, literal, and clear reading of the text demonstrated God's approval—nay, insistence upon!—slavery. How is it that the Bible is very "clear" on something at one point in history, then clearly the opposite a century later?

Perhaps because the "literal" and "clear" interpretation may actually depend on the readers' frame of reference more than on the wording of the text itself. Both literal and symbolic interpretations may be skewed by the readers' bias,[26] and both ways of reading can be safeguarded similarly. First, interpretations should derive directly from the text under consideration, in its context, and in comparison with similar Scriptures (see the example that follows here). Second, Christian exegesis should always be done with reference to Christ, as suggested by Luke 24:27.

Literalists claim that medieval allegorizing harmed the church, but in fact, almost all ancient symbolic interpretations were based on these safeguards. Over and over, the commentaries of the Early Middle Ages point the reader to Christ and extol various virtues of the Savior. This hardly did any disservice to the Christian faith; rather, the more-than-literal readings of the Bible served to bolster Jesus' centrality in spiritual life.

There's a third safeguard against readers' bias: any true interpretation should promote obedience to the greatest commands—love of God and neighbor. Augustine put this eloquently in his *Confessions*:

> See how stupid it is, among so large a mass of entirely correct interpretations which can be elicited from these

> words, to rashly assert that a particular one has the best claim to Moses' view, and by destructive disputes to offend against charity itself, which is the principle of everything he said in the texts we are trying to expound.[27]

In other words, if we argue over interpretations and harm others in so doing, we've got it wrong even if we get it right!

An Example of Symbolic Bible Reading: Mark 10:46–52

An obvious place to begin contemplation of this text's symbolism is the word "blind." A scan of that term throughout the Scriptures reveals a number of similar healing stories, but also a weighty number of passages where blindness / loss of sight is used symbolically, indicating either spiritual or judicial blindness. (Compare Deut. 16:19, 1 Sam. 12:3, Prov. 28:27, Mt. 5:29, Mt. 6:23, Mt. 18:9, and Luke 6:39.) Blindness, therefore, was a common metaphorical device, both among Jews and early Christians.

Reading the broader setting around this passage affirms the metaphorical sense of blindness in the story, one that's both spiritual and moral in nature. The healing of Bartimaeus is preceded by conflicts with religious teachers (9:38–41, 42–49, 10:1–12), and then the spiritual blindness of Jesus' own disciples (10:35–45). Matthew, writing shortly after Mark, will condemn the Pharisees who oppose Jesus as "blind guides" (chapter 23). Bartimaeus' healing is followed by multiple pronouncements of judgment on those who refuse to see God's truth in their midst (Mark 11:12–25, 27–33, and 12:1–12). All this is leading up to the ultimate case of blindness toward justice, which is Jesus' false trial, torture, and execution, in chapters 14–15.

In contrast with all the symbolic blindness around him, Bartimaeus, despite opposition from those around him, knows to call out to Jesus: "Many rebuked him and told him to be quiet, but he called out all the more, 'Son of David, have mercy on me!'" (verse 48). Having noted the themes of spiritual blindness and faith, this verse represents the opposition to discipleship that Jesus' followers in every age must face. In fact, Bartimaeus' confession is so perfect that it has been used (with the substitution of "God" for "David") for centuries as the "Jesus Prayer."

The passage ends with another evocative phrase, one that surely held a breadth of meaning in the writer's mind: he "followed Jesus on the way" (the Greek word *odos* meant "path, road, journey"). In the first century, "Christian" was rarely used to refer to Christ's followers; instead, the common designation was "people of the way" (Acts 9:2). So this passage is a complete narrative of one man's conversion. He was spiritually blind, not unlike many of his fellows; then he called out to Jesus, asking for Divine mercy, despite the castigation of his peers; Jesus transformed him, bringing illumination; and finally, Bartimaeus entered into the community of believers, committing his life to the ongoing journey of discipleship.

Where a physically grounded reading yielded interesting but hardly applicable facts about physical blindness, a metaphorical approach models the way that Christ transforms lives. Like Bartimaeus, we can recognize our places of darkness, we can call for Christ to touch us, we can be illuminated, and we can then embark on a lifelong path among the company of Jesus' followers. With the addition of "second-dimension" reading, we see the larger pattern of the peacock's plumage in this text.

Notes

1. Thomas O'Loughlin, *Journeys on the Edges: The Celtic Tradition* (New York: Maryknoll, 2000), 36–37.

2. Ibid., 39–40.

3. Bible scholars are uncertain that Paul of Tarsus actually wrote all of the epistles that bear his name, so I limit examples to those books deemed undeniably Pauline.

4. Michael Graves, *The Inspiration and Interpretation of Scripture: What the Early Church Can Teach Us* (Grand Rapids, MI: Eerdmans, 2014), Kindle edition, location 1088.

5. Eric A. Seibert, *Disturbing Divine Behavior: Troubling Old Testament Images of God* (Minneapolis, MN: Fortress Press, 2009),63.

6. Ibid.

7. Ibid.

8. Kenton L. Sparks, *God's Word in Human Words: An Evangelical Appropriation of Critical Biblical Scholarship* (Grand Rapids, MI: Baker, 2008), 28.

9. Ian Bradley, *Following the Celtic Way: A New Assessment of Celtic Christianity* (London: Darton, Longman and Todd, 2018), 124.

10. Anglandicus, "Cummian's Commentary on Mark," May 17, 2012, http://anglandicus.blogspot.com/2012/05/cummians-commentary-on-mark.html. [Accessed November

19, 2015.]

11. Ibid., "Aileran the Wise: Commentary on the Genealogy of Jesus," May 27, 2012, http://anglandicus.blogspot.com/2012_05_01_archive.html. [Accessed November 19, 2015.]

12. George Aichele, *Sign, Text and Scripture: Semiotics and the Bible* (London: Bloomsbury T&T Clark, 1997), 11.

13. Huston Smith, *The Soul of Christianity: Restoring the Great Tradition* (San Francisco: Harper, 2005), 19, 23. Italics are Smith's.

14. Quoted by Philip Zaleski & Carol Zaleski in *The Fellowship: The Literary Lives of the Inklings,* (New York: Farrar, Straus and Giroux, 2015), 182.

15. C. S. Lewis, *The Inspirational Writings of C.S. Lewis: Surprised by Joy, Reflections on the Psalms, The Four Loves and The Business of Heaven* (New York: International Press, 1991), 187.

16. Ibid., 200.

17. Marcus J. Borg, *The Heart of Christianity: Recovering a Life of Faith* (San Francisco, Harper, 2003), 49.

18. ———, *Jesus: Uncovering the Life, Teachings, and Surprising Relevance of a Spiritual Revolutionary* (San Francisco: HarperOne, 2008), HarperCollins e-books location 927. (Italics in the original.)

19. Graves, Kindle location 2916.

20. Philip Jenkins, *Laying Down the Sword: Why We Can't Ignore the Bible's Violent Verses* (New York: HarperCollins, 2011), 13.

21. Ibid., 210.

22. Ibid., 57.

23. Graves, Kindle location 1091.

24. Ibid., Kindle location 2914.

25. N. T. Wright, "How Can the Bible Be Authoritative?" http://ntwrightpage.com/Wright_Bible_Authoritative.htm. [Accessed Nov. 27, 2015.] The Laing Lecture, 1989, and the Griffith Thomas Lecture, 1989, originally published in *Vox Evangelica*, 1991, 21: 7–32.

26. Postmodern Bible interpreters increasingly point to the question of whether interpretations come from the perspective of privilege or that of the dispossessed. Racial minorities, women, people of other religions, and LGBTQ persons have historically been on the receiving end of disempowering interpretations.

27. Saint Augustine, *Confessions: A New Translation by Henry Chadwick* (New York, Oxford University Press, 1992), 265.

SEVEN

The Third Dimension

Imagining

There are almost innumerable . . . drawings
if you take the trouble to look very closely,
and penetrate with your eyes
to the secrets of the artistry,
you will notice such intricacies,
so delicate and subtle, so close together,
and well-knitted . . . so fresh still in their colorings
that you will not hesitate to declare
that all these things must have been
the result of the work, not of men, but of angels.

—Gerald of Wales, 1185, describing the Book of Kells

For over a thousand years, the Book of Kells has evoked praise and wonder. Its full-page illuminations require a contemplative gaze. First, you see the large design, like the gilded frame of a picture or the form of a carpet. Then, looking closer, you discern portraits: a large letter, an animal, or a human figure. Gazing more closely, a third dimension is apparent: a seemingly infinite maze of knotwork, geometric patterns, dots of bright color, and lines so small they could only be drawn using a magnifying stone. "The decorative scheme of the entire Book of Kells," wrote Georgetown Professor John Pfordresher, "is thus a single, repeating visual metaphor for a theological reality that has ever subtler, even deeper levels of organization and meaning."[1]

In the Gospel of Matthew section, the Book of Kells presents a stunning full-page portrayal of Christ, enclosed within a lavish frame of swirls and geometric patterns. Jesus gazes at the viewer and holds a large, bright red book on his knee. This image of the Bible is central to the entire page; the eye is drawn to it immediately. To the left and the right of Christ's head are a mirrored pair of peacocks. Each sits atop a chalice filled with grapes—the Eucharist. Their tails are cascades of bright colors in intricate design.

What do these peacocks represent? The peacock, which annually sheds and then re-grows its glorious train, is a time-honored Christ symbol. These peacocks may also, on the other hand, signify the Bible, the image of which is so prominent on this page. We recall Eriugena's peacock analogy and the fact that Eriugena shared the same Irish monastic background as the scribes who made the Book of Kells.

Pfordresher explained the connection between the imaginative art of the Book of Kells and the Celtic approach to Scripture:

> For the Iona community, God's book was mysterious, never to be fully comprehended. Rather than seeking one, single meaning for a word or a sentence, this tradition prized multiplicity, layers of meaning, expecting a complexity and richness beyond the limits of any one reading. . . . The imaginative response to this in the Book of Kells is the analogous complexity of its ornamentation, functioning as a visual metaphor for the value presumed inherent in the text.[2]

Another example of Celtic illuminated Scriptures, the Lindisfarne Gospels, expressed the multiplicity of meanings inherent in the text by another device: mixing alphabets. Michelle Brown wrote, "These pages feature letters of Latin, Greek, Runic, and Ogam inspiration."[3] The very shape of letters could be revelatory; for example the Greek capital Delta (Δ) might be used in place of the Latin letter D in *Deus*, signifying the fact that God is always Three-in-One (the triangle is a symbolic representation of the Trinity). This multiplicity of signifiers in a text reminded the reader that there were layers of meaning in every passage—layers that pointed to the hidden depths of God's Being.

This third dimension of Celtic Bible interpretation differs from the levels of grounded and symbolic readings in that it consciously seeks to go *beyond* meanings found in the text itself. After the hard work of asking, "What does the text say?" the reader proceeds to speculative questions—"What might be left unsaid?" "What happened before and after the story?"—and then on to the really vital question: "What does this say to us, here and now?"

For the Celts, God is ultimately a mystery; there will always be Divine secrets beyond human kenning. At a certain point, physical realities serve only as a portal to the infinite. The only way to pass that entryway is to travel by imagination.

While the "grounded" and "symbolic" levels of Bible interpretation were common to almost all Christians throughout the world in the Early Middle Ages, this third level of imaginative interpretation does seem uniquely Celtic—at least in the degree to which it was practiced. This may be due in part to the Celts' love of story.

Storytelling has been a benchmark of Celtic cultures from at least the early Iron Age. The Bards were the most honored members of Celtic society; they were greater than kings, since a good singer-storyteller could raise another man up to become king—or cast him down in disrepute. Living in colder regions, Celtic societies depended on their tale-tellers to keep each village and clan inspired through the long, perilous winters. Wordsmiths were honored as much as blacksmiths, and they were just as essential for the community's survival.

Creative forms of expression possess a raw power, activated by our ancestral instincts. As George Aichele wrote:

> For members of an oral culture, poetic language, like the speech of God in Genesis 1, casts a spell over reality. The

> poet's words are true because they make things real—they create reality. The powerfully spoken (or "winged") words of the poet cannot be denied.[4]

Perhaps the Celts took to the Bible so readily because its stories are derived from oral tellings—and the Celts, coming straight to Christianity from an oral culture, understood Scripture accordingly.[5]

The literalist may be disappointed to realize that the Bible is to such a large degree comprised of story. Far from being "God's little instruction book" it is "God's enormous storybook." For the Celts this was not a drawback—quite the opposite. Stories had shaped their lives since the Bronze Age. Stories gave them power and pride; stories enabled them to overcome all manner of deadly foes. Stories were the very blood that ran in Celtic veins, and the early Celtic Christians were filled with wonder and delight to have so many stories about the King of Mystery and his people.

Professor Ian Bradley, in his recent book *Following the Celtic Way: A New Assessment of Celtic Christianity*, wrote, "The Celtic saints were associated with an approach to expressing and explaining the mysteries of the Christian faith through story, symbol, and verse rather than through intellectual proposition." They did so because they "assimilated and adopted the Celtic druidic, bardic approach of emphasizing the affective and poetic over the cognitive."[6]

As soon as Christians arrived in Celtic lands with the gospel, the art of storytelling was applied to the life-giving narratives of the new Christian faith. Writings such as *Altus Prosator (The High First-Sower), In Tenga Bithnua (The Ever-New Tongue),* and *Saltair Na Rann (The Psalter of the Quatrains)* fuse bardic storytelling skills with Bible narratives, resulting in uniquely Celtic works of adoration to God. These do not claim to be scriptural commentary; they are works of imagination inspired by the Scriptures that proceeded on a trajectory beyond them.

The High First-Sower, allegedly composed by Columba, is written in Latin with uniquely Celtic phraseology. For instance, the word in the title, *Prosator*, is literally "the first one to sow," a term from Gaelic farming. Poetic in form, *Altus Prosator* has a stanza for each letter of the alphabet, a form perhaps inspired by similar biblical psalms. Its subject is the great work of God, from Creation to Judgment. Such an epic theme requires all the varied skills of human creative writing, and the *Altus Prosator* does not disappoint; images sourced from the Bible, Christian apocrypha, bardic Nature poems, and Greek mythology weave together in a paean of Divine praise. Describing the flood, the narrative invokes "the swelling whirlpools of Cocytus, covered by Scyllas"—references to Greek mythology.[7] Moses' ascent of Mount Sinai is retold with dramatic concrete imagery:

> Who has ascended Mount Sinai to speak with the Lord, has heard the thunder sounding exceedingly and the noise of the great resounding trumpet, has seen the lightning flashing in a ring and lights and missiles and crashing stones, save Moses, judge of the people of Israel?[8]

From the earthly plane, the narrator lifts the reader to heaven where "in the fervent resounding chanting of hymns by thousands of angels flourishing in their holy dances . . . the Trinity receives threefold praise eternally."[9]

The Ever-New Tongue is an even more creative work, written in Irish. "Far from simply being a commentary on the testimony of the Bible," wrote John Carey, "it purports to be a separate heavenly revelation, unveiling all the mysteries of the universe."[10] Allusions are drawn from the Bible, Gnostic writings, travel literature, gemology, and astronomy, but, said Carey,

> its contents have been transformed in the crucible of the author's imagination to become part of his own unique, fantastic vision of reality. *In Tenga Bithnua* is, indeed, one of the most remarkable examples . . . of that inspired fusion of learning and creativity which distinguishes so much of early Irish literature.[11]

The central theme—the universal revelation of Divine utterance—is echoed today by the motto of the United Church of Christ, "God is still speaking." And the very first words reflect the majesty of this tale:

> The High King of the world, who is mightier than every king, who is loftier than every power, who is fiercer than every dragon, who is gentler than every child, who is brighter than suns, who is holier than every elder, who is

> more vengeful than men, who is more loving than every mother, the only Son of God the Father, bestowed this account upon the many peoples of the world, concerning the world's form and creation.[12]

The epic is filled with lovely imaginative details such as this comment on the creation of humanity: "And there is in it material from the sun and the stars of heaven also; so that is what makes the brightness and light in people's eyes."[13] This insight not only charms; it is scientifically true, for, as Carl Sagan said, "We are made of starstuff."[14] *The Ever-New Tongue* also reveals that the entirety of the universe was originally contained "in the round many-shaped aggregation of the material of the world . . . in the round many-shaped mass from which the world was extracted,"[15] a phrase evocative of the singularity that physicians posit before the Big Bang.[16] The symphony of creation's beauty ends with an invitation to eternal glory "where the good has not been lacking, and is not lacking, and will never be lacking," and the exhortation, "May we all reach that kingdom, may we deserve it, may we dwell in it world without end, Amen."[17]

The Psalter of the Quatrains is another example of imaginative extrapolation from Scripture. "In the process of putting the Bible story into medieval Irish verse, it transforms it and imbues it with an Irish flavor," Carey wrote.

> The *Saltair* gives us an unparalleled opportunity to look at the panorama of the Scriptures through the eyes of the tradition to which this book is devoted; and to experience some of the vivid, colourful, imaginative sensibility which that tradition brought to the church's teachings.[18]

It interweaves Hellenistic legend with New Testament imagery: "That is virginal Olympus without movement or stir, according the noble account of the ancient sages; its name is 'the third holy heaven.'"[19] And there are unique Celtic phrases, such as "the King of every splendid substance, our mighty tree."[20] Also in this work, God is "the bright King of mysteries," a fitting title in a poetic work that aims to lift the reader into the realm of the numinous.

These imaginative writings defy categorization in the Christian literary traditions; perhaps they could be characterized as Celtic *Midrash*, the ancient rabbinic commentary on the Hebrew scriptures that is attached to the biblical text. The comparison may seem strange at first: what did the Gaels and the Jews have in common back in the Early Middle Ages? But it is not far-fetched. "In the virulently anti-Jewish world of the sixth to eighth centuries," Herren and Brown note, "the British and Irish Churches preserved a deep regard for the most Jewish aspects of Christianity."[21]

Like the Celts, Jewish interpreters expected their scriptures to yield multiple levels of meaning and diverse interpretations. Furthermore, they expected God to *continue* speaking through the Torah. Rabbi Sandy Eisenberg Sasso explains that by "grounding themselves in the biblical narrative," Midrash

> retold the ancient story in the light of new realities and changing conditions. . . . The Rabbis said that when God revealed the Ten Commandments at Sinai, not only the Exodus generation stood at the foot of the mountain, but all generations of Israel yet to come. They believed that revelation did not take place once upon a time but all the time.[22]

The Continuing Relevance of the Celts' Imaginative Reading

> Customarily, when we read the Bible we listen to its ancient words, allowing it to tell us our ancestors' stories. But what would it mean to read the Bible by allowing it to help us tell the stories of *our* lives? What if we read our joys, our fears, and our doubts into the biblical narrative?[23]

Rabbi Eisenberg Sasso's invitation for readers to create their own Midrash can also serve as our call to engage in Celtic Midrash—imaginative reading of Scripture.

This might be considered the *application* stage of Celtic Bible study, but it goes beyond the way some modern interpreters use that word. Too often the Bible is reduced to the role of "God's rulebook," a moral and spiritual instruction manual. In the Celtic view, however, the peacock-beauty of Scripture is more than merely instructional; the Celtic imaginative approach beckons us to draw wonder and inspiration from the Bible, transforming us into Christ-likeness. This is not the old cliché question, "What would Jesus do?" but rather, "What *is* Jesus *doing now* within human beings and the world?"

When we read with imagination, we directly engage with the Bible as narrative (in other words, *story*)—and story is the most powerful form of communication. As Andover Newton Professor of Bible Gregory Mobley explains, stories are potent because they fill a fundamental human need for mastery over chaos: "Once we have a story, we have direction, shape, motive. . . . We no longer have chaos, we have meaning and order. And the story we create will represent this meaning and order." He goes on to say that from our very beginnings,

> Humans are storytellers, meaning-makers, and pattern-tracers. Even before we learn to count, we are constantly putting two and two together, tying episodes together into the daisy-chain cause-and-effect sequences we know as stories.[24]

Studies show that our brains acquire new information more effectively through narratives, and reading stories makes us more prone to compassionate behavior. An article in the *Harvard Business Review* concludes:

> When you want to motivate, persuade, or be remembered, start with a story of human struggle and eventual triumph. It will capture people's hearts—by first attracting their brains.[25]

Perhaps the power of narrative, coupled with our capacity to imagine, can provide a new understanding of the Bible's relevance. While the Bible continues to work in a strictly literalist sense for many Christians today, many others struggle with the Scriptures. The Bible leads some to faith, but for others it is a stumbling block in faith's way. Embracing the Bible as narrative may provide us with a renewed handle on the Bible's value and authority. As N. T. Wright writes,

> Authority is not the power to control people, to crush them, and keep them in little boxes. The church often tries to do that—to tidy people up. Nor is the Bible as the Vehicle of God's authority meant to be information for the legalist.[26]

The Bible's greater "authority" is that of inspiration, largely imparted in the form of stories. Again quoting Wright:

> Story authority, as Jesus knew only too well, is the authority that really works. Throw a rule book at people's head, or offer them a list of doctrines, and they can duck or avoid it, or simply disagree and go away. Tell them a story, though, and you invite them to come into a different world; you invite them to share a world-view or better still a "God-view." . . . Stories determine how people see themselves and how they see the world. Stories determine how they experience God, and the world, and themselves, and others. Great revolutionary movements have told stories about the past and present and future. They have invited people to see themselves in that light, and people's lives have been changed. If that happens at a merely human level, how much more when it is God himself, the Creator, breathing through his word.[27]

The Scriptures do indeed possess life-changing power—the power of inspiration. "Inspiration" can be trivialized to holiday cards or cheerful little tabloid stories, but the word can also convey the consuming fire of the Spirit setting mortals ablaze with purpose and passion. An oft-cited verse declares that "every Scripture is inspired by God" or, as more literally translated in the World English Bible, "every Scripture is God-breathed" (2 Timothy 3:16). The text refers to Genesis 2 when God created Adam and "breathed into his nostrils the breath of life." So the Bible's own claim to inspiration is not primarily about having all the facts straight or providing the best set of rules; inspiration is the *imparting of life.*

The Scriptures are meant to transform us, so that we can say, "It is no longer I who live but Christ living in me" (Galatians 2:2). To this end, God calls us through both the book of Nature and the books of Scripture. As we engage the Bible with our imagination, we allow our souls to be filled with God's breath, transforming us into the Divine nature (2 Peter 1:4).

An Example of Imaginative Reading: Mark 10:46–52

Imaginative reading can be deep and powerful, and especially so when it is your own imagination at work. As Greg Mobley wrote, "The task of theology is the linking of our individual story to the biggest story we can imagine,"[28] and only you can link God's story to your own.

To that end, I've suggested the following three steps. I know it's tempting to skip over the exercises in a book—but I believe it will benefit you to take time for contemplation as suggested here. Doing so will enable you to firm up in your mind what you've learned so far and—most important—help you to connect your story to God's story.

1. Reread Mark 10:46–52.

2. Imagine yourself as Bartimaeus—or, alternatively, as a bystander to this incident. Be as sensual as you can while imagining the scene, keeping in mind that you are blind at the beginning of the story. What does the air feel like against your face? What do you smell? What do you hear? Pay close attention to your emotions as you perceive the messages your senses bring you.

3. Now connect the story of Bartimaeus with memories that are your story. When have you felt the kind of feelings that the story invokes in you? What story would you tell along with this one? *Imagine how this story can alter your story* as it unwinds into the future.

For the Celts, the Bible was something amazing and wondrous. Like the world of Nature, it was to be "read" attentively, with the commitment and fascination the lover feels for the beloved. In today's world, where reading is done purely for pleasure or information, we have lost the knack of reading with the Celts' passionate, open receptivity to Mystery, the immense larger and deeper Reality that underlies all life.

But that approach to reading Scripture is not lost to us. With practice, we too can learn to open our hearts and minds to the gift of the Divine Word. When we do, we will find that it enters us as the Breath of God, inspiring us and transforming us in unpredictable ways—and then sweeping through us like a flame that kindles new life and healing in the world around us.

Notes

1. John Pfordresher, *Jesus and the Emergence of Catholic Imagination* (Mahwah, NJ: Paulist, 1998), 221.

2. Ibid., 220.

3. Michelle P. Brown, "Southumbrian Book Culture: The Interface Between Insular and Anglo-Saxon," in Colum Hourihane, *Insular & Anglo-Saxon: Art & Thought in the Early Medieval Period* (Princeton, NJ: Princeton University Press, 2011), 31.

4. George Aichele, *Sign, Text and Scripture: Semiotics and the Bible* (London: Bloomsbury T&T Clark, 1997), 10.

5. For an outstanding treatment of the entire Bible in light of storytelling form, see Gregory Mobley, *The Return of the Chaos Monsters—and Other Backstories of the Bible* (Grand Rapids, MI: Eerdmans, 2012).

6. Ian Bradley *Following the Celtic Way: A New Assessment of Celtic Christian* (London: Darton, Longman and Todd, 2018), 50.

7. John Carey, *King of Mysteries: Early Irish Religious Writings* (Dublin: Colour Books, 2000), 40.

8. Ibid., 44.

9. Ibid., 47.

10. Ibid., 75.

11. Ibid.

12. Ibid., 77.

13. Ibid., 79.

14. Carl Sagan, *Cosmos* (New York: Random House, 2011), 115.

15. Carey, 81.

16. On the website *Universe Today*, Frasier Cain writes, "The scientific consensus is that the Universe is expanding, having gotten its start in a single point 13.7 billion years ago. . . . But what came before the Big Bang? Since all matter and energy was tangled up into a single point of infinite volume and density, it's hard to imagine how you could look to a time before that. Cosmologist Martin Bojowald and others from Penn State University thinks it's possible. . . . According to Bojowald, a mathematical technique called Loop Quantum Gravity, which combines relativity and quantum mechanics, gives a different view of the early Universe. Instead of being infinitely small and dense, it was compacted down into a ball of some volume and density . . . very similar to the space-time geometry we have in our current Universe. (http://www.universetoday.com/2026/before-the-big-bang-2/#; accessed September 12, 2016.)

17. Carey., 96.

18. Ibid., 97.

19. Ibid., 102.

20. Ibid.

21. Herren and Brown, 109.

22. Sandy Eisenberg Sasso, *Midrash: Reading the Bible with Question Marks* (Brewster, MA: Paraclete Press, 2007), 7, 37.

23. Ibid., 3.

24. Gregory Mobley, *The Return of the Chaos Monsters—and Other Backstories of the Bible* (Grand Rapids, MI: Eerdmans, 2012), Kindle location 109.

25. Paul J. Zak, "Why Your Brain Loves Good Storytelling," *Harvard Business Review*, October 28, 2014, https://hbr.org/2014/10/why-your-brain-loves-good-storytelling/. [Accessed November 30, 2015.].

26. N. T. Wright, "How Can the Bible Be Authoritative?" *Vox Evangelica* 1991, 21, 7–32.

27. Ibid.

28. Mobley, Kindle location 116.

Blessing

My prayer is that reading the Bible the Celtic way will offer you a new journey of adventure and wonder.

May you gaze upon the peacock's feathers:
iridescent, shimmering, dazzling.

May you see the many ways—
indeed an infinite number—
of interpreting the Scriptures.

May your reading be threefold:
grounded,
symbolic,
and with imagination.

May you read with the Trinity:
with the High First-Sower,
with the King of Mysteries,
with the Divine Breath filling you.

May your reading restore all that is broken in you,
and may you know
Christ within you,
the Beloved Community around you,
holy Earth beneath you.
AMEN

Suggested Readings

On Celtic Christianity

Adomnán of Iona: ***Life of St Columba*** (Penguin Books). The life of the Saint, grouped by categories of miracles, written by the ninth abbot of Iona. An entryway into the thinking of a Celtic Christian in the heyday of the Iona Monastery.

Bede: ***The Ecclesiastical History of the English People*** (Penguin Books). The first English history book. Bede displays grudging admiration for his Celtic brethren and records numerous events of the Early Middle Ages that would otherwise be unknown.

Robert Boenig: *Anglo-Saxon Spirituality: Selected Writings: Classics of Western Spirituality* (Paulist Press). The similarities between Celtic and Anglo-Saxon Christians in the Early Middle Ages far outweigh the differences; they reflect a common Insular outlook. This is the best single volume of translated Anglo-Saxon documents.

Thomas Cahill: *How the Irish Saved Civilization: The Untold Story of Ireland's Heroic Role from the Fall of Rome to the Rise of Medieval Europe* (Doubleday). Popular history, written like a novel, and a good first introduction to Celtic Christianity for many readers.

John Carey: *King of Mysteries: Early Irish Religious Writings* (Four Courts Press). Along with Davies' *Celtic Spirituality* (below), the best source of translated Celtic Christian documents.

Paul Cavill: *Anglo-Saxon Christianity: Exploring the Earliest Roots of Christian Spirituality in England* (Fount). A professor of Old English mixes translated documents with his own Christian insights. If you enjoy *Water from an Ancient Well* (McIntosh) or *Celtic Christianity* (Simpson), you will also benefit from this book.

Oliver Davies: *Celtic Spirituality: Classics of Western Spirituality* (Paulist Press). A treasure trove of translated primary documents, nicely explained and arranged.

Leslie Hardinge: *The Celtic Church in Britain* (Teach Services). Hardinge did a formidable amount of research, unfortunately marred by being dated and by his denominational biases. Nonetheless, this book contains valuable information not found elsewhere.

Michael W. Herren and Shirley Ann Brown: *Christ in Celtic Christianity: Britain and Ireland from the Fifth to the Tenth Century* (Boydell Press). Written on a scholarly level, combining analysis of written and artistic expressions, the authors argue that there was a distinctly Celtic Christology in the Early Middle Ages, largely due to the continuing influence of Pelagius.

Meg Llewellyn: *Celtic Miracles and Wonders: Tales of the Ancient Saints* (Anamchara Books). You can almost hear the voice of a bard relating these folktales of the saints. An easy-to-read and fun introduction to the ethos of Celtic Christianity, with brilliant short introductions.

Kenneth McIntosh: *Water from an Ancient Well: Celtic Spirituality for Modern Life* (Anamchara Books). Father Richard Rohr called this a "fine book" that "allows us to rediscover the depth and wisdom of Celtic Christianity."

Thomas O' Loughlin: *Celtic Theology: Humanity, World and God in Early Irish Writings* (Continuum). Written on a scholarly level, this is a deeper, richer treatment of the themes in *Journeys on the Edges* (below). Valuable if you have already read the more basic books in this list.

Thomas O'Loughlin: *Journeys on the Edges : The Celtic Tradition: Traditions of Christian Spirituality Series* (Orbis Books). A neglected gem and "must" reading for anyone interested in Celtic Christianity. O'Loughlin is unusual insofar as he is professor at the Centre for the Study of Religion in Celtic Societies, University of Wales (so he works vocationally with primary materials) *and* he writes this book in simple language for laypeople, with the aim of spiritual guidance. This book is unique in its combination of sober scholarship and spiritual discernment.

Edward C. Sellner: *Wisdom of the Celtic Saints* (Ave Maria Press). An excellent, popular-level overview of the chief Celtic Saints (and a few lesser known) with a fine set of introductions to Celtic Christianity.

Ray Simpson: *Celtic Christianity: Deep Roots for a Modern Faith* (Anamchara Books). Ray Simpson is one of the founders of the Community of Aidan and Hilda. This is one of the finest overviews, aimed to spiritually enrich the reader, on Celtic Christianity.

Ray Simpson: *The Celtic Book of Days: Ancient Wisdom for Each Day of the Year from the Celtic Followers of Christ* (Anamchara Books). This is a daily devotional with insights from Scripture and the lives of the Celtic saints for each day of the year.

Lilly Weichberger & Kenneth McIntosh: *Brigid's Mantle: A Celtic Dialogue Between Pagan & Christian* (Anamchara Books). Diana Greenfield, Church of England New Age Apologist, wrote, "As someone who seeks to stand on the bridge between Pagans and Christians, I found the concept of Brigid's Mantle as the cloak under which we can meet both helpful and inspiring."

On the Bible

Raymond E. Brown: *An Introduction to the New Testament* (Doubleday). Despite being somewhat dated, this may be the best overall New Testament introduction. The late Raymond Brown was a foremost expert in New Testament studies, combining his vital Christian faith with outstanding scholarship, resulting in this finely balanced work. Brown has the rare honesty and wisdom to distinguish between what is known and what can only be conjecture, enabling him to make statements or pose questions as appropriate.

Common English Bible. A recent translation that combines simple language with careful translation choices. Unlike most translations, the CEB retains ambiguity where the texts in the original languages defy easy understanding. The translation team consists of members from a broad variety of Christian denominations, ensuring that the translation is free from theological bias.

Michael D. Coogan, Editor: *The New Oxford Annotated Bible* (Oxford University Press). The go-to general-purpose study Bible, from a mainline Christian perspective, with commentary by top-notch scholars.

Sandy Eisenberg Sasso: *Midrash: Reading the Bible with Question Marks* (Paraclete Press). A rabbi presents this fun, easy-to-read introduction to Jewish Bible interpretation, including "how to" sections.

Peter Enns: *The Bible Tells Me So . . . Why Defending Scripture Has Made Us Unable to Read It* (HarperOne). A Professor of Biblical Studies explains how he re-learned the value of the Bible after struggling with it. If the Bible has never seemed like a stumbling block to you, you don't need this book; but if you are struggling with doubts about the Scriptures, this could be valuable.

Harry Y. Gamble: The New Testament Canon: Its Making and Meaning (Wipf and Stock). A brief but scholarly guide to this very complex topic.

Gregory Mobley: *The Return of the Chaos Monsters—and Other Backstories of the Bible* (William B. Eerdmans). Mobley, Professor of Bible at Andover-Newton Seminary, presents an absolute treasure trove. He shows how the entire Bible is better understood when heard as storytelling. The medium suits the message, as

Mobley's exquisite prose seems more like poetry. This book may revolutionize the way you read Scripture.

Celtic Christianity

Deep Roots for a Modern Faith

The world of the long-ago Celts appeals to many of us in the twenty-first century. Whether we are looking to find our cultural heritage or are seeking an alternative to worn and restrictive religious forms, the Earth-centered, woman-friendly, inclusive faith of the Christian Celts offers us a deep-rooted alternative approach to traditional Christianity. The Celts experienced "thin places," where they sensed the supernatural world; they honored their poets, singers, and artists; and they passionately followed the Christ of the Gospels. Theirs was a church without walls, which lived naturally and comfortably within the community. Ray Simpson has spent most of his life walking in the footsteps of the Christian Celts, and now he allows us to experience for ourselves their dynamic spirituality.

Paperback Price: $24.95

Kindle Price: $8.99

Brigid's Mantle

A Celtic Dialogue Between Pagan and Christian

Long ago, the story goes, Brigid flung out her mantle over the world. Beneath its shelter, the Earth and its people could find healing, insight, and growth. Using this as their central metaphor, the authors—one a Pagan healer and the other a Christian minister—engage in a dialogue that is ultimately about what it means to be spiritual, to be a person of faith. With Brigid, as both a Pagan Goddess and a Christian saint, at the center of their dialogue, the authors first provide the historical foundation for the Celtic culture, past and present. They build on this a concept of Celtic spirituality that embraces the arts, Nature, the supernatural world, compassion for those in need, and gender equality.

Paperback Price: $14.95

Kindle Price: $5.99

Water from an Ancient Well

Celtic Spirituality for Modern Life

Using story, scripture, reflection, and prayer, this book offers readers a taste of the living water that refreshed the ancient Celts. The author invites readers to imitate the Celtic saints who were aware of God as a living presence in everybody and everything. This ancient perspective gives radical new alternatives to modern faith practices, ones that are both challenging and constructively positive. This is a Christianity big enough to embrace the entire world.

Paperback Price: $24.95

Kindle Price: $7.49

Anamchara Books

AnamcharaBooks.com

Printed in Great Britain
by Amazon

35843323R00085